Social*Text* 130

Collateral Afterworlds: Sociality besides Redemption

Edited by Zoë H. Wool and Julie Livingston

Anne Allison is professor of cultural anthropology at Duke University. A specialist in contemporary Japan, she has written about gender, hostess clubs, corporate capitalism, popular culture, Pokemon, and precarity. Her books include *Nightwork: Sexuality, Pleasure, and Corporate Masculinity in a Tokyo Hostess Club* (1994), *Millennial Monsters: Japanese Toys and the Global Imagination* (2006), and *Precarious Japan* (2013).

Naisargi N. Dave is associate professor in the Department of Anthropology at the University of Toronto. She is the author of *Queer Activism in India: A Story in the Anthropology of Ethics* (2012). Her second book is tentatively titled *The Social Skin: Humans and Animals in India.*

Angela Garcia is associate professor of anthropology at Stanford University. She is the author of *The Pastoral Clinic: Addiction and Dispossession along the Rio Grande* (2010) and is writing a book on therapeutic violence in Mexico City.

Fady Joudah is a practicing physician of internal medicine. His poetry and translations have earned him several national and international awards, among them the Yale Series prize, a PEN Award, a Griffin Poetry Prize, and a Guggenheim Fellowship.

Julie Livingston is professor of social and cultural analysis and history at New York University. She is the author of *Improvising Medicine: An African Oncology Ward in an Emerging Cancer Epidemic* (2012) and *Debility and the Moral Imagination in Botswana* (2005). She has been a member of the *Social Text* collective since 2007.

Elizabeth A. Povinelli is Franz Boas Professor of Anthropology and Gender Studies at Columbia University. She is the author of five books, the latest of which is *Geontologies: A Requiem to Late Liberalism* (2016). She is also director of three Karrabing Film Collective films.

Solmaz Sharif is currently a lecturer at Stanford University. Her first book of poems, *Look*, was published in 2016.

Lisa Stevenson is associate professor and William Dawson Scholar in the Department of Anthropology at McGill University. She is the author, most recently, of *Life beside Itself: Imagining Care in the Canadian Arctic* (2014). Stevenson is a medical and visual anthropologist whose research has focused on contemporary and historical forms of care in the Canadian Arctic.

Zoë H. Wool is assistant professor of anthropology at Rice University, where she is also a core faculty member in the medical humanities program and an affiliate of the Center for the Study of Women, Gender, and Sexuality. Her first book, *After War: The Weight of Life at Walter Reed* (2015), was awarded honorable mention for the 2016 Gregory Bateson Prize.

Collateral Afterworlds

An Introduction

Zoë H. Wool and Julie Livingston

A Litany

I remember him falling beside me,
the dark stain already seeping across his parka hood.
I remember screaming and running the half mile to our house.
I remember hiding in my room.
I remember that it was hard to breathe
and that I kept the door shut in terror that someone would enter.
I remember pressing my knuckles into my eyes.
I remember looking out the window once
at where an ambulance had backed up
over the lawn to the front door.
I remember someone hung from a tree near the barn
the deer we'd killed just before I shot my brother.
I remember toward evening someone came with soup.
I slurped it down, unable to look up.
In the bowl, among the vegetable chunks
pale shapes of the alphabet bobbed at random
or lay in the shallow spoon.
—Gregory Orr

During a recent discussion of the defining ordeal of his life—the hunting accident in which at age twelve he unintentionally shot and killed his younger brother—the American poet Gregory Orr noted that trauma, violence, and death shatter meaning.[1] In the disorienting aftermath of this tragedy his parents each retreated into their own torment, as did Orr in his terror and alienation. Orr eventually found his way to poetry, to art, which have sustained but not, in his words, "healed" him. His poetry is a

DOI 10.1215/01642472-3727960 © 2017 Duke University Press

struggle toward meaning but not a story of redemption, or a testimonial to the strength of family and community in the face of grievous harm.

This special issue of *Social Text* takes up the all too timely problem of meaninglessness, ethical disorientation, and the insufficiency of social life across contexts tied together by a pervasive sense of precarity and relentless uncertainty that puts meaning and the social itself in question. We suggest that such afterworlds are characteristic of a broader historical moment characterized by the proliferation of disasters that are lived as endemic conditions: mass extinctions,[2] infrastructural ruin,[3] national economic and geopolitical failure,[4] the legal and scientific sanctioning of state torture and murder,[5] unprecedented displacements of those seeking refuge from war, poverty, and the drying up or flooding out of life possibilities,[6] even the end of the hospitality of the very earth itself.[7] Activists, activist-scholars, and revolutionaries may seek to transform the disasters of the present into a rock-bottom or dialectical turning point from which a better world will rise. But our effort here is to convey something of the lives and worlds that endure out of the way of such redemptive possibilities—not beyond their reach but that roll along off to the side of efforts to stabilize, repair, and improve any collective lot in the name of the future. These are collateral afterworlds, marked especially by the temporality of a difficult present where life is unhinged from the pervasive hope for a better tomorrow.[8] In them, we seek to examine chronic, ongoing experiences in which sociality fails to redeem experiences of injury, vulnerability, and loss. In doing so we ask how and why people act toward themselves and others in contexts where such redemption is not recognized as immanent or expected as forthcoming. How do people take up or sidestep the problem of being, in contexts where they enjoy neither a progressive telos nor a radical political vision to orient their efforts and offer hope of meaningful futures? How do these efforts remind us (yet again) of the falsity of assuming any clear divide between the worlds of the living and the dead, the ontological status of being and not being?

Because of this very challenge to meaning that Orr describes, rupture, schism, and violence have long been a particular fascination for those of us with an interest of one sort or another in the warp and weft of a social fabric. The *social* in *Social Text* marks a major center of gravity in political and academic thought. The dual problems of accounting for social coherence and social change have animated many of the founding moments of social theory. And yet our current political moment, like the era that birthed academic social science, is simultaneously characterized by the paradoxical relationship of endemic suffering and narratives of social progress (albeit a progress now in jeopardy). As such, it calls for renewed attention to the problematic vicissitudes of social relationships, their uneven valuation, and their ethical entailments. How is it that a mode of living, a social world, endures, accommodates, or is disintegrated by what appear to be crises? What if the very existence of that social world is toxic, threatening, such that isolation rather than proximity is sought? What happens to sociality as it unfolds in spaces of slow death?[9] What genres of entextualization are available to us as critical scholars seeking to get a hold on how these precarious worlds are lived and died? Orr stood as a child at the center of a terrible personal accident, a tragedy, a fluke powerful enough to unravel his world entirely. What about worlds in which such experiences of loss and alienation reflect the steady state of social and political life? In the US context, these questions are being powerfully taken up in thinking about the necropolitical disregard for black bodies and lives, as well as a host of brown, queer, and disabled ones newly targeted by the current regime.[10] Our inquiry dovetails with that one and also extends it geographically and analytically, exploring different national and biopolitical locations and raising questions about the implications for the concept of the social, questions that find a unique articulation when grounded ethnographically, as we describe below.

The essays collected here explore experiences of living in collateral afterworlds—sites of disaffection and stasis in the shadow of large-scale political and economic forces. From Inuit teenagers living in the suicidal detritus of settler colonialism in northern Canada (Stevenson) to Mexican drug addicts whose families had them kidnapped to closed, informal institutions as a form of treatment in Mexico City (Garcia), these are experiences that are poorly accounted for by a full faith in the hope of the social, and by "strong theories" of historical, social, or cultural change.[11] Through an ethnographic fidelity to the uneven textures of life, we question how to make sense of the social in the absence of a tightly focused vision of human life as properly and collectively sustained by agglutinating forces of community, kin, or other reliable and iterative superorganic social forms. It is not that social life is absent (as if it could ever be) but, rather, that the familiar alliance of sociality with social and biological life and of fragmentary solitude with social and biological death doesn't quite fit.

Our return to the "everyday" of *Social Text* conjoins us as ethnographers and anthropologists to the journal's interdisciplinary public,[12] and we write both within and at odds with anthropology as social science. Anthropology has a many-storied history—orientalist phantasmagoria, handmaiden of colonialism,[13] epistemologically, materially, and psychically invested in the "savage slot."[14] Through careful, anxious, angry, and sometimes mournful reflection on this legacy, the discipline has become more attuned to the power and politics of knowledge, becoming a key voice in calls to provincialize and provisionalize knowledge.[15] Anthropology's particular contributions to these discussions have emerged largely from the centrality of ethnography to our discipline, a practice that comprises both dwelling and writing.[16]

And yet, the commitment to meaning, to a patterned coherence, continues to orient the discipline. What to do, then, with contexts of profound precarity, such as that Orr describes, in which the chronic instability of meaning is essential to the experience? Anthropology is currently grappling with the implications of this question for itself as a discipline.[17] But this is also where we think ethnography, unbound from strict limits of a disciplinary conversation, might have something more to offer. As a broad range of critical thinkers take up urgent questions about the necropolitics and debility currently proliferating across zones and conditions of dispossession, abandonment, and vulnerability,[18] we suggest ethnography—with its ability to sit amid the intimacies of the everyday—might be a valuable inflection point for critical analysis. The small acts and complex feelings that make up vulnerable or lonely lives are not merely building blocks of "gigantic histories," be they of trauma or resilience.[19] We suggest that, even as everyday life registers the divisions of contemporary necropolitics, it would behoove us to insert some friction into any analytic desires to slot precarious life into grand narratives of history.

The forces of colonialism, capitalism, and their various complexes clearly condition the zones of life described in the contributions to this issue of *Social Text*. Yet by attending to the incommensurabilities and confounding potentialities of life and death within them, the authors collected here encounter ethical spaces of the ordinary that are *not* fully captured by grand narratives of social change and do not have a proper part within the division of the sensible that would make them known as good or bad for, or even part of, any larger social project at hand. The common senses and accompanying ethics discerned in these ethnographies are porous, open-ended, and decidedly small scale. In their varied forms, the contributions here endeavor to find ways not so much of writing worlds (as anthropology might have it)[20] but of conveying discordances, full of fragments, sounds, affects, images, gestures, ghosts, and memories, maintaining their ambivalence and interrogating their significance while keeping meaning undecided. The knowledge project of ethnography written in this mode is one that, like the particular forms of poetry we have included, push back on the foreclosure of meaning, insisting that "we *are* more than we *know*."[21]

We see the concept of the social as the place where many disciplinary conversations and legacies converge. It is also the place where our attention, as anthropologists, to the politics of writing knowledge and, as ethnographers, to the difficulty of meaning in the midst of precarity might open up the most productive questions across a wider range of modes of inquiry. As Elizabeth Povinelli suggests in the afterword to this issue, one "reason to dwell critically in these spaces is simply to insist that their existence have a public. And this insistence that these spaces be able to claim space within the public of critical thought is indeed increasingly necessary given the forms of institutional erasure arising from the intersection of legal preemption and liberal 'protection.'" Another is "to show that the condition of life within these spaces provides a critical perspective on the formation of late liberal power" and, we would add, the concept of the social that subtends other efforts at this same critical project.

In thinking through the widespread scholarly investment in the force of the social, we want to point out two things. First, while anthropologists, ethnographers, historians, and others attending to human experience under the sign of the social have long felt free to think past the holism of the foundational social sciences of the nineteenth and early twentieth centuries, we retain, perhaps of necessity, a legacy of something we might call social integralism. This term marks a loyalty to the integrity of the magic math that makes people (and their metaphysical companions—ancestral shades, nonhuman animals, things, plants, and other matter) add up, and add up to more than the sum of their parts; to a culture, a way of life, a historically situated social world. Boundaries might be contested, but as such they nonetheless mark worlds. Even within the Manchester school of social anthropology, which put internal conflict and renegotiation at the center of social life, there is the comforting promise of renewal and the reproduction of a dynamic and fraught but thereby cohesive world.[22] Social relations may break down or be systematically wanting (as went the perverse logic of the Moynihan Report), but they remain the fetish on which so many hopes are pinned. This social integralism is perhaps the most fundamental of Durkheimian gifts and not one that is easily refused. Yet we posit here that some modes of writing experience might better keep the question open.

Second, there is a certain alliance between biological life and social life inherent in this integralism, one that sees sociality as bound to biological life and social disintegration as bound to biological death, such that at the level of one particular life—the life of one person, say—social death and biological death run together. There is obviously both truth and significance to this. We ought not ignore or deny, for example, the many ways that colonial interventions into indigenous forms of sociality continually produce new forms of violence and death,[23] or the ways that late modern sovereignty hinges on the social interplay of death, killing, and terror,[24] or the ways that the social death of the prison, the asylum, and the nursing home produce biological vulnerability.

And yet, the insistence on the vitality of social life, and the binary opposition of life and death, suspends the substantial body of feminist, anthropological, and historical work that interrupts such a metaphysics, revealing this opposition to be but yet another of modernity's folk idioms.

Indeed, ethnography, like that collected here, is increasingly sensitive to the ways that life and death, ruin and resurgence, comprise ever present "waxing and waning intensities."[25] The fact is that many people live not in spaces of vitality or in the face of imminent death but in lasting zones of precariousness, temporalities of impasse or slow death,[26] or within the continuous present tense.[27] Even as experts and governors deploy machineries and logics of crisis on their behalf,[28] such conditions do not, indeed cannot, raise alarms beyond the sort that Orr evokes for the people existing in them. The blood seeps, the ambulance comes, someone brings a bowl of soup, a world is fragmented, and so it goes. Family, community, and kin are insufficient, absent, and at times deadly, yet nonetheless imperative. Our aim here is to work against the false dilemma that emerges in social theory between vital forms oriented toward the future and the unproductive dead ends of a toxic or melancholic present. That these are two sides of the same coin is precisely what we mean by collateral afterworlds. And so we seek to examine and to narrate how people go about acting in that in-between space, the place of circularity, of enforced idleness.

Let us be clear: it is not our aim to vacate the social as a meaningful category. Personhood is inherently relational; so too is ecology. Rather, we refuse to assume the durability or depth of a world that is shared, or the instability or thinness of a world that is not. Instead, we take these as ethnographic questions. We are interested in registering all sides of the contradictions of care, obligation, and investment that shape such worlds and their conjoined aspects of "for better" and "for worse."

There are important echoes of queer theoretical debates about the antisocial thesis here, and also of queer efforts to make worlds amid an epidemic. Many Japanese, for example (see Allison's contribution in this issue), are remaking their social attachments both in life and in death as marriage and workplace are eroding as the dominant social anchors. Broadening our scope, we might understand such queer interventions as part of a minor history of sociality and decay in social theory to which we seek to contribute the ethnographic texture of the contemporary.[29] To do this, we trace world-making attachments that ambivalently crisscross being with others, being alone, and being with death, as well as varied kinds of others to whom attachment may count as ethically significant, from dogs and maggots to intensely copresent strangers, dreamt familiars, and even corpses. As we trace these attachments through daily life across continents, classes, institutions, and genres, we hope to give an emergent sense of these afterworlds as ethical spaces, even as we see how the coordinates of the social that usually direct ethical investment are disoriented and unsteady.

Here, our experiments with and across genre are especially important. The contributions mix evocative ethnography, philosophy, and social theory in diverse ways and bring film and other archives into the space of ethnography. In part, this is an attempt to convey the "difficulty of reality" that ethnography can render[30] and to refuse the convenient fiction that the meaning of worlds appears in coherent fashion even to its most astute observers. Ethnography has a long relationship with poetry, especially those forms that seek to register the disorientations of lived moments and disrupt our ability to diagnose a situation or to know precisely what has happened or what it means.[31] Such writing, ethnographic and poetic, attends to the dreamlike and the sensory activity through which the social world is lived while remaining anchored in experience. Particularly important to our effort to register the characteristics of such labor of life in the contemporary moment, this writing conveys a sense of the uncertain temporalities and patterns that characterize the unintended collateral effects created by liberal yearning toward the good life. These gaps themselves are constitutive of rather than contra the social fabric, equal to any seemingly reliable threads of kinship, affiliation, memory, or law that supposedly make it hold. The poems in this collection push us to reflect on those gaps in meaning, reflecting how history and biography intrude to make a moment feel both small and supervalent (Sharif, "Planetarium"; Joudah, "Thank You") and questioning the sources of meaning that subtend authoritative archives of life and death (Joudah, "Footnotes").

Ethnography, a mode of writing-dwelling that is in itself inherently, awkwardly social, is particularly well suited to such tasks, especially when it grounds itself in the haze, even the incomprehensibility, of experience.[32] In this mode, the political romance of human endurance and resilience falls away in the ambiguous texture of the collateral afterworld. Sticking close to experience helps slow the rush to transform endurance into transcendence, keeping hope in abeyance without insinuating the meaninglessness of worlds that are not suffused with it.

Such ethnography also allows the question of meaning to reappear in various guises, not least of which is a consistent attention to the forms of life and life-forms worthy of living at all. The people we encounter here do not find answers to that question but are feeling out ways of being and not being in relation to it: lonely citizens of a Japan whose ways of death have been undone by economic collapse (Allison); Mexican families whose forms of care uncannily redouble the violence of drug wars that have put them at risk (Garcia); Inuit generations whose accounts of time are full of ghost voices speaking into the aporia of colonial silence and death (Stevenson); Indian animal workers who minister to death-bound life (Dave); injured American soldiers whose precarious investment in the present is tethered to impossible fantasies of the future (Wool).

By positioning our collected ethnographies under the heading of collateral afterworlds, we focus our attention on the fact that modes of sociality, forms of life, and ethical investments that have nothing to offer liberalism's continually failing vision of a better tomorrow are accorded little value by those who continue to romanticize social integralism. Their relegation—through targeted action or active neglect—to social and material spaces of worthlessness is justified in a language that speaks, full of hope, in the future anterior tense.[33] Historians have upended the telos of progress that authorizes such divisions, and we wish to pursue the implications of the metaphysics of a stalled present on sociality itself.[34] The ethnographic worlds we explore here are structured by such efforts to clean up the mess of liberal governance, culling forms of life (and death) that are perceived as threatening or that are not legible as worthy. In these worlds, such forms of life may be salvaged, but they may also remain unruly, unpromising, and ambivalently situated somewhere off to the side of dominant good-life imaginaries of the future. Our explorations, therefore, home in on a different tense, that of endurance in which life goes on and on amid the damage, regardless. Pustule-riddled and starving stray dogs may be dewormed on the open streets of Delhi (Dave) only to carry on the same. Wounded US Army veterans may be "rehabilitated" at Walter Reed Army Medical Center (Wool) only to be shed by the military "family." Meanwhile, the production of such forms of life continues apace.

This temporal vantage point is crucial, which is again where ethnography provides insight. Crisis moments seem at first glance to be moments like Orr's: instances in which it seems the social might fall apart, in which ritual fails to reinstantiate meaning. But the diagnosis of those moments on a broad scale as crises belongs, as Janet Roitman notes,[35] to a particular historical ontology, one shared by forms of modern liberal expertise from the social sciences to public policy. The diagnosis is itself a practice of making history, conforming narrative to its salvific telos. While such a diagnosis has many effects on those living within it, it also has the effect of abridging the protracted moment of living they are in. Crisis, that is, is an attempt to cleave before from after. The present becomes nothing more than a fault line. Yet Orr, like many of the interlocutors engaged in this collection of essays and poems, would have us know that time can stretch and loop; the present can be relentless.

Crisis is invoked as a moment when the truth is laid bare, as a moment of revelation. But the worlds the authors pursue here are made up of uncertainties, ambivalent meaning, and the quotidian unfolding of many chronic and acute destabilizations of life, akin to and as unique as Orr's. Mothers, wives, and children taken away without warning (Stevenson); bodies and worlds upended by war (Wool); murdered neighbors, relatives, and friends (Garcia); animals dramatically killed, cared for, and let live or die (Dave); reclusive, hermetic children and isolated, lonely seniors (Allison). Taken together, they pattern the present into something far more persistent than a fault line beyond which lies a revelatory after in which meaning is reanchored. While these moments and spaces may, in other circumstances, be considered as evidence of crisis, we consider them here as emplotted in a rather different temporality:[36] the temporality of the afterworld, the wake, the slow space, a stickiness left by the structural and, yes, more historic shifts that created these conjunctures of instability, of precarity.

There is no revelatory truth we are after here. While this collection characterizes some of the collateral effects of our recent moment of liberal optimism (a moment that has now been superseded by the rise of a new global authoritarianism and plutocracy), it also aims to help us think through a broader set of irresolvable tensions within scholarly considerations of the social.[37] Such tensions have been present in other epochs, where they have been narrated and ethically accounted without liberalism's progressive telos. But in our current moment these tensions take their "untimely" force[38] from the way they muddle the telos of social emergence—the very telos that so many students of the social (and narrators of crisis) tend to find comforting.

In those stories of social emergence, sociality, that mode of being bonded with others, offers hope for (human) communities to come.[39] Sociality is vested with special value, sometimes through its ability to make social forms endure, sometimes through its ability to produce enduring social transformations. As the force of that magic math that aggregates and secures life into the wholly social, sociality promises to buoy people across contemporary landscapes in which even the rock bottom of life threatens to be turned to quicksand. But, in the shadow of social integralism, there is also an increasing sense by many that we must both twist and multiply our modes of attention. Social and political enfranchisement may hang itself on the bareness of life;[40] a superpower can compulsively restage its own destruction to "constitute pleasure and national community";[41] optimism can be cruel;[42] care can be violent;[43] violence can be domestic.

One axis revealed by ethnography that we pursue across these essays is physical proximity. What are its effects, its possibilities? The sensory dimensions of sociality—haptic, aural, visual, kinesthetic—upon which proximity's immediacy is constituted distort, fray, and vanish across space, producing relief, loss, or some combination of the two. When Indian activists touch wounded, rotting animals (Dave), when a Japanese monk insists that he will only communicate face-to-face (Allison), proximity becomes an end in itself. When an Inuktitut voice recording of a mother removed to a colonial sanatorium travels the unbridgeable distance between her body and that of her child, the absence of proximity is the wound that kills (Stevenson). When rain deluges Mexico City and urbanites huddle together under awnings in fleeting moments of proximity, the city briefly coheres (Garcia). Yet that same physical copresence can overwhelm and stress into the visual and sensory exposures of mutual confinement or surveillance (Garcia) that may secure life even as they exacerbate its discomforts. The essays collected here further suggest that the gap that emerges across space is such that words may not hold their meaning and that reconfigurations of distance and proximity may condense meaning in ways too potent for some to tolerate (Wool, Stevenson, Allison). Attention to such modes of being with others, of viscerally experiencing the intensities that make up a moment in a world, analytically sharpens our sense of the fragility of forms of relationality—especially kinship—that we might usually count on for systematic social mapping.

The ethnographies collected here thereby extend recent attention to zones of precarious living where abandonment, withdrawal, severance, and solitude might seem to place life at the very boundary of the social.[44] In such zones, a social imagined as having been durable, knowable, fecund, and densely populated may now be imagined as destabilized by violence, rupture, and crises both endemic and acute.[45] Figured as ethical thresholds where the value and limits of life are rendered questionable, existing registers of ethical attachment seem to collapse, suggesting the decomposition of populations into an inscrutable and unwieldy multiplicity of solitudes. Life is made to teeter precariously on the verge of becoming and unbecoming.

And yet, explorations of even the starkest of such verges show we are wise to slow the jump from thin or indiscernible sociality to utter failure and social death. Recognition and intimacy can be grounded in or eked out of suffering, victimhood, violence, or death.[46] Solitude can capacitate shared sexuality.[47] Ethical attachments may arise within and across apparent ontic or species divides.[48] Such attachments may prove fickle, but also flexible and capacious, invigorating new forms and values of life while leaving others to rot.[49] Sociality abides, sometimes hopefully, sometimes toxically, always multivalent, in the thinnest spaces of life.

Rather than judge the relative success or failure of social worlds, the essays collected in this issue of *Social Text* ask about what attachments and disconnections do. What are the affective attachments and ethical entailments of being with others in spaces where the life-sustaining bonds of sociality are strained or contorted by necropolitics, the politicization of life, and seductive forms of death-bound subjectivity? What are the stakes and ambivalent meanings of being in common with others when the coherence of community is illusive, undesirable, or iatrogenic?

We take up these questions across a range of sites, each with its own collateral position in the wake of contemporary promises and deferments of the good life. Naisargi Dave plunges into the indistinctions of ethics of human and animal suffering in India; Lisa Stevenson ponders what it means to send one's voice across spaces of death wrenched open by colonial histories and legacies for Inuit in northern Canada; Anne Allison explores the problem of burial among lonely Japanese; Zoë Wool unfolds the vital and "in-durable" sociality among wounded American soldiers; and Angela Garcia explores an ethical horizon where violence is enfolded in care among addicts in Mexican drug treatment *anexos*. We conclude where we began—with poetry. Solmaz Sharif travels across the dream space between shared marvel and war where the sky is a locus of longing, violence, and a military occupation of the senses that repeats itself across life span and history. Fady Joudah opens up the uncertainties of death that medical knowledge would suture. He poses metatextual questions that redouble problems of historiography and meaning, blurring the epitaph and footnote, pushing us to consider the unstable meaning of deaths and what it might mean to know them well. He captures impossible intimacies given voice in the echoing of sacred texts read with gratitude across the bodies of cadavers.

Notes

1. Orr, "When a Child Kills."

2. Dawson, *Extinction*; Kolbert, *Sixth Extinction*.

3. Allison, "Reflections on Welfare"; Adams, *Markets of Sorrow, Labors of Faith*. See also Anne Allison's contribution in this issue.

4. Lewis, *Big Short*; Roitman, *Anti-crisis*; Varoufakis, *And the Weak Suffer What They Must?*

5. Khalili, *Time in the Shadows*; Hajjar, *Torture*; Soldz et al., *All the President's Psychologists*.

6. De León, *Land of Open Graves*; Lucht, *Darkness before Daybreak*; Dewachi et al., "Changing Therapeutic Geographies."

7. Nixon, *Slow Violence*; Chakrabarty, "Climate of History"; Scranton, *Learning to Die in the Anthropocene*.

8. See Povinelli, *Economies of Abandonment*.

9. Berlant, "Slow Death."

10. See, e.g., Taylor, *From #BlackLivesMatter to Black Liberation*; Coates, *Between the World and Me*; and Winters, *Hope Draped in Black*. For a global black position and radical vision, see Moten and Harney, *Undercommons*.

11. Sedgwick, "Paranoid Reading," 133–36.

12. Edwards, "*Social Text*."

13. Said, *Orientalism*.

14. Trouillot, "Anthropology and the Savage Slot."

15. Chakrabarty, "Postcoloniality"; Clifford, *Partial Truths*.

16. Clifford and Marcus, *Writing Culture*; see also Povinelli, *Economies of Abandonment*.

17. Robbins, "Beyond the Suffering Subject."

18. Haritaworn, Kuntsman, and Posocco, *Queer Necropolitics*; Puar, *Terrorist Assemblages*; Weheliye, *Habeas Viscus*.

19. Ko, *Cinderella's Sisters.*

20. Abu-Lughod, *Writing Women's Worlds.*

21. Cohen, "Gut Wisdom."

22. See, e.g., Turner, *Schism and Continuity.*

23. Povinelli, *Empire of Love*; Fassin, "Humanitarianism as a Politics of Life." See also Stevenson's contribution in this volume.

24. Mbembe, "Necropolitics."

25. Das and Han, *Living and Dying*, 30; Tsing, *Mushroom at the End of the World.*

26. Berlant, *Cruel Optimism.*

27. Povinelli, *Economies of Abandonment.*

28. Fassin and Pandolfi, *Contemporary States of Emergency*; Ticktin, *Casualties of Care*; Roitman, *Anti-crisis.*

29. See, e.g., Lingis, *Community*; Lingis, *Deathbound Subjectivity*; Eng and Kazanjian, *Loss*; and Butler, *Precarious Life.*

30. Diamond, "Difficulty of Reality"; see also Stevenson, *Life beside Itself*, 31.

31. See Rosaldo, *Day of Shelly's Death.*

32. See, e.g., Stewart, *Ordinary Affects.*

33. Povinelli, *Economies of Abandonment*, 12–13.

34. Palmie, "Historicist Knowledge"; Koselleck, *Futures Past*; Schoenbrun, "Conjuring the Modern in Africa"; and Sewell, *Logics of History.*

35. Roitman, *Anti-crisis.*

36. Stewart, "Trauma Time"; Stewart, *Ordinary Affects.*

37. Arendt, *Human Condition.*

38. Rabinow, "Foucault's Untimely Struggle."

39. Biehl and Locke, "Deleuze and the Anthropology of Becoming."

40. Fassin, *When Bodies Remember.*

41. Masco, "Engineering the Future."

42. Berlant, *Cruel Optimism.*

43. Mulla, *Violence of Care.* See also Angela Garcia's contribution in this issue.

44. See, e.g., Allison, *Precarious Japan.*

45. See, e.g., Biehl, *Vita*; and Chua, *In Pursuit of the Good Life.*

46. See, e.g., Garcia, *Pastoral Clinic.*

47. Coleman, "Being Alone Together."

48. See, e.g., Bennett, *Vibrant Matter*; Kohn, *How Forests Think.*

49. See, e.g., Povinelli, *Empire of Love*; Tsing, *Mushroom at the End of the World.*

References

Abu-Lughod, Lila. 1993. *Writing Women's Worlds: Bedouin Stories.* Berkeley: University of California Press.

Adams, Vincanne. 2013. *Markets of Sorrow, Labors of Faith: New Orleans in the Wake of Katrina.* Durham, NC: Duke University Press.

Allison, Anne. 2013. *Precarious Japan.* Durham, NC: Duke University Press.

Allison, Anne. 2016. "Reflections on Welfare from Postnuclear Fukushima." *South Atlantic Quarterly* 115, no. 1: 175–81.

Arendt, Hannah. 1998. *The Human Condition.* 2nd ed. Chicago: University of Chicago Press.

Bennett, Jane. 2010. *Vibrant Matter: A Political Ecology of Things.* Durham, NC: Duke University Press.

Berlant, Lauren. 2007. "Slow Death: Sovereignty, Obesity, and Lateral Agency." *Critical Inquiry* 33: 754–80.

Berlant, Lauren. 2011. *Cruel Optimism*. Durham, NC: Duke University Press.

Biehl, João. 2005. *Vita: Life in a Zone of Social Abandonment*. Berkeley: University of California Press.

Biehl, João, and Joshua Locke. 2010. "Deleuze and the Anthropology of Becoming." *Current Anthropology* 51, no. 3: 317–37.

Butler, Judith. 2004. *Precarious Life: The Power of Mourning and Violence*. New York: Verso.

Chakrabarty, Dipesh. 1992. "Postcoloniality and the Artifice of History." *Representations* 37: 1–26.

Chakrabarty, Dipesh. 2009. "The Climate of History: Four Theses." *Critical Inquiry* 35, no. 1: 197–222.

Chua, Jocelyn. 2014. *In Pursuit of the Good Life: Aspiration and Suicide in Globalizing South India*. Berkeley: University of California Press.

Clifford, James. 1986. "Introduction: Partial Truths." In *Writing Culture: The Poetics and Politics of Ethnography*, edited by James Clifford and George Marcus, 1–26. Berkeley: University of California Press.

Clifford, James, and George Marcus, eds. 1986. *Writing Culture: The Poetics and Politics of Ethnography*. Berkeley: University of California Press.

Coates, Ta-Nehisi. 2015. *Between the World and Me*. New York: Spiegel and Grau.

Cohen, Ed. 2013. "Gut Wisdom, or Why We Are More Intelligent Than We Know." *Somatosphere.org*. 21 October. somatosphere.net/2013/10/gut-wisdom-or-why-we-are-more-intelligent-than-we-know.html.

Coleman, Leo. 2009. "Being Alone Together: From Solidarity to Solitude in Urban Anthropology." *Anthropological Quarterly* 82, no. 3: 755–77.

Das, Veena, and Clara Han, eds. 2014. *An Anthropology of Living and Dying in the Contemporary World*. Berkeley: University of California Press.

Dawson, Ashley. 2016. *Extinction: A Radical History*. New York: OR Books.

De León, Jason. 2015. *The Land of Open Graves: Living and Dying on the Migrant Trail*. Oakland: University of California Press.

Dewachi, Omar, Mac Skelton, Vinh-Kim Nguyen, Fouad M. Fouad, Ghassan Abu Sitta, Zeina Maasri, and Rita Giacaman. 2014. "Changing Therapeutic Geographies of the Iraqi and Syrian Wars." *Lancet* 383, no. 9915: 449–57.

Diamond, Cora. 2003. "The Difficulty of Reality and the Difficulty of Philosophy." *Partial Answers: Journal of Literature and the History of Ideas* 1, no. 2: 1–26.

Edwards, Brent Hayes. 2009. "*Social Text*." *Social Text* 27, no. 3: 231–34.

Eng, David L., and David Kazanjian. 2003. *Loss*. Berkeley: University of California Press.

Fassin, Didier. 2007. "Humanitarianism as a Politics of Life." *Public Culture* 19: 499–520.

Fassin, Didier. 2007. *When Bodies Remember: Experiences and Politics of AIDS in South Africa*. Berkeley: University of California Press.

Fassin, Didier, and Mariella Pandolfi. 2010. *Contemporary States of Emergency: The Politics of Military and Humanitarian Interventions*. New York: Zone Books.

Garcia, Angela. 2010. *The Pastoral Clinic: Addiction and Dispossession along the Rio Grande*. Berkeley: University of California Press.

Hajjar, Lisa. 2013. *Torture: A Sociology of Violence and Human Rights*. New York: Routledge.

Haritaworn, Jin, Adi Kuntsman, and Silvia Posocco, eds. 2013. *Queer Necropolitics*. London: Routledge.

Khalili, Laleh. 2012. *Time in the Shadows: Confinement in Counterinsurgencies*. Stanford, CA: Stanford University Press.

Ko, Dorothy. 2005. *Cinderella's Sisters: A Revisionist History of Footbinding*. Berkeley: University of California Press.

Kohn, Eduardo. 2013. *How Forests Think: Toward an Anthropology beyond the Human*. Berkeley: University of California Press.

Kolbert, Elizabeth. 2014. *The Sixth Extinction: An Unnatural History*. New York: Henry Holt.

Koselleck, Reinhardt. 2004 (1979). *Futures Past: On the Semantics of Historical Time*. Translated by Keith Tribe. 2nd ed. New York: Columbia University Press.

Lewis, Michael. 2011. *The Big Short: Inside the Doomsday Machine*. New York: Norton.

Lingis, Alphonso. 1989. *Deathbound Subjectivity*. Bloomington: Indiana University Press.

Lingis, Alphonso. 1994. *The Community of Those Who Have Nothing in Common*. Bloomington: Indiana University Press.

Lucht, Hans. 2012. *Darkness before Daybreak: African Migrants Living on the Margins in Southern Italy Today*. Berkeley: University of California Press.

Masco, Joe. 2013. "Engineering the Future as Nuclear Ruin." In *Imperial Debris: On Ruins and Ruination*, edited by Ann Laura Stoler, 252–86. Durham, NC: Duke University Press.

Mbembe, Achille. 2003. "Necropolitics." Translated by Libby Meintjes. *Public Culture* 15, no. 1: 11–40.

Moten, Fred, and Stefano Harney. 2013. *The Undercommons: Fugitive Planning and Black Study*. New York: Minor Compositions.

Mulla, Sameena. 2014. *The Violence of Care: Rape Victims, Forensic Nurses, and Sexual Assault Intervention*. New York: New York University Press.

Nixon, Rob. 2011. *Slow Violence and the Environmentalism of the Poor*. Cambridge, MA: Harvard University Press.

Orr, Gregory. 2014. "When a Child Kills: Reflections on a Shooting Range, from One Who Knows." *New York Times*, 29 August.

Palmie, Stefan. 2013. "Historicist Knowledge and Its Conditions of Impossibility." In *The Social Life of Spirits*, edited by Ruy Blanes and Diana Espiritu Santo, 218–39. Chicago: University of Chicago Press.

Povinelli, Elizabeth. 2006. *The Empire of Love*. Durham NC: Duke University Press.

Povinelli, Elizabeth. 2011. *Economies of Abandonment: Social Belonging and Endurance in Late Liberalism*. Durham, NC: Duke University Press.

Puar, Jasbir. 2007. *Terrorist Assemblages: Homonationalism in Queer Times*. Durham, NC: Duke University Press.

Rabinow, Paul. 2009. "Foucault's Untimely Struggle: Toward a Form of Spirituality." *Theory, Culture, and Society* 26, no. 6: 25–44. dx.doi.org/10.1177/0263276409347699.

Robbins, Joel. 2013. "Beyond the Suffering Subject: Toward an Anthropology of the Good." *Journal of the Royal Anthropological Institute* 19, no. 3: 447–62. dx.doi.org/10.1111/1467-9655.12044.

Roitman, Janet. 2013. *Anti-crisis*. Durham, NC: Duke University Press.

Rosaldo, Renato. 2013. *The Day of Shelly's Death: The Poetry and Ethnography of Grief*. Durham, NC: Duke University Press.

Said, Edward. 1979. *Orientalism*. New York: Random House.

Schoenbrun, David. 2006. "Conjuring the Modern in Africa: Durability and Rupture in Histories of Public Healing between the Great Lakes of East Africa." *American Historical Review* 111, no. 5: 1403–39.

Scranton, Roy. 2015. *Learning to Die in the Anthropocene: Reflections on the End of a Civilization*. San Francisco, CA: City Lights Books.
Sedgwick, Eve Kosofsky. 2003. "Paranoid Reading and Reparative Reading, or, You're So Paranoid, You Probably Think This Essay Is about You." In *Touching Feeling: Affect, Pedagogy, Performativity*, 123–51. Durham, NC: Duke University Press.
Sewell, William H. 2005. *Logics of History: Social Theory and Social Transformation*. Chicago: University of Chicago Press.
Soldz, Stephen, Nathaniel Raymond, Steven Reisner, Scott A. Allen, Isaac L. Baker, and Allen S. Keller. 2015. *All the President's Psychologists: The American Psychological Association's Secret Complicity with the White House and US Intelligence Community in Support of the CIA's "Enhanced" Interrogation Program*. assets.documentcloud.org/documents/2069718/report.pdf.
Stevenson, Lisa. 2014. *Life beside Itself: Imagining Care in the Canadian Arctic*. Berkeley: University of California Press.
Stewart, Kathleen. 2005. "Trauma Time: A Still Life." In *Histories of the Future*, edited by Daniel Rosenberg and Susan Harding, 321–39. Durham, NC: Duke University Press.
Stewart, Kathleen. 2007. *Ordinary Affects*. Durham, NC: Duke University Press.
Taylor, Keeanga Yamahatta. 2016. *From #BlackLivesMatter to Black Liberation*. Chicago: Haymarket Books.
Ticktin, Miriam. 2011. *Casualties of Care: Immigration and the Politics of Humanitarianism in France*. Berkeley: University of California Press.
Trouillot, Michel-Rolph. 1991 "Anthropology and the Savage Slot: The Poetics and Politics of Otherness." In *Recapturing Anthropology: Working in the Present*, edited by Richard G. Fox, 17–44. Santa Fe, NM: School of American Research Press.
Tsing, Anna Lowenhaupt. 2015. *The Mushroom at the End of the World: On the Possibility of Life in Capitalist Ruins*. Princeton, NJ: Princeton University Press.
Turner, Victor. 1957. *Schism and Continuity in an African Community*. Manchester: Manchester University Press.
Varoufakis, Yanis. 2016. *And the Weak Suffer What They Must? Europe's Crisis and America's Economic Future*. New York: Nation Books.
Weheliye, Alexander G. 2014. *Habeas Viscus: Racializing Assemblages, Biopolitics, and Black Feminist Theories of the Human*. Durham, NC: Duke University Press.
Winters, Joseph Richard. 2016. *Hope Draped in Black: Race, Melancholy, and the Agony of Progress*. Durham, NC: Duke University Press.

Greeting the Dead

Managing Solitary Existence in Japan

Anne Allison

Even Tokyo slows down during O-bon, the season of greeting and revisiting the dead. It is August 2013, and the day feels still as my friend Maia and I head to a cemetery at the edge of the city. She has asked me to accompany her, as the thought of going alone is unsettling. Once death and the dead were part of everyone's everyday. People died at home, were buried in or close to rice fields outside, and became spirits enshrined in household altars that the living communed with on a daily basis. But now, and particularly in the cities, people rush about and concentrate their energies on other things. Less tethered to the land and to the ancestors buried there, Japanese have left death to the experts: funerary companies and the Buddhist priests at the temples where families, at least those that have them, keep their family plots. When someone dies, a family contracts with a funerary company to handle the body and services and contacts the priest at the Buddhist temple where they are parishioners to preside at the wake. The expense has become exorbitant, an average of $14,000 for the funeral alone.[1] And for its handling of the dead—the only time or service for which many turn to religion at all during their lives—Buddhism becomes known as "the religion of death," an unseemly association, tinged by the money that temples/priests earn in the process.

On this day the temple is quiet. We are the only visitors to the cemetery, and Maia finds the grave she is seeking with ease. As she anticipated, the plot is unkempt—the telltale sign of neglect by those family members who should be tending it (a wife and son, in this case). "Just as I suspected," she says under her breath, as she greets the friend who is buried there: a former colleague with whom she ran a business for years. Clapping her hands and bowing her head, she quickly sets upon straight-

DOI 10.1215/01642472-3727972 © 2017 Duke University Press

ening things up. She pulls weeds and pours water over the stones in front of the grave site. Speaking softly, she tells her friend about recent events at the business and how she's been doing herself. The flowers she has brought are put in stone vases on the grave, and the incense and candles are lit in the box altar underneath. A few more weeds are pulled, and the stones in front of the grave are swept again. Finally, looking purposeful, Maia claps her hands, bows her head, and claps once more. I follow her lead, and then we walk off. The visit has been good, and Maia tells me she is happy she has come. But it's not exactly her place to be tending to the grave, as the priest keeps telling her. Yet her friend's wife and son don't do their duty. And Maia bears her own guilt in not being more attentive to her friend when, after the Lehman Shock of 2008 almost wiped out their business, he fell into a deep depression. When he committed suicide, he was all alone. Maia was the one who discovered the body three days later.

The rate of suicide went up in 1998 during the "lost decade" of economic decline. It stayed at 32,000–33,000 deaths per year until 2012, when it started to slowly decline. Men are twice as likely as women to commit suicide, driven overwhelmingly by problems related to finances and work. Despite its prevalence, however, suicide is not something people easily discuss. It still carries a stigma—the reason, I assume, that Maia has shared the story of her friend's suicide with very few people. But suicide is not the only form of socially troubling death these days. Another is the phenomenon much in the news lately of what is called lonely or solitary death (*kodokushi, koritsushi*)—persons who die alone and whose bodies are discovered days or weeks after the fact. As reported by Japan's national broadcasting system in its January 2010 television special on Japan's "relationless society" (*muen shakai*), there were 33,000 such deaths in 2009—a number eerily consistent with that of suicide. When such bodies go unclaimed by their families, an increasingly common circumstance, the remains get sent to Buddhist temples, where they are placed in communal plots for the socially disconnected (*muenbotoke*). A sign of abandonment and eternal solitude, this is an unenviable state—becoming a relationless Buddha (or soul).

Leaving the cemetery, we see the plot assigned the displaced dead. In this corner of the graveyard, labeled *muenhaka*, the grass is overgrown, and there are no offerings of any kind. Most cemeteries have these plots, and, as I was told earlier in the summer when headed to check one out in my neighborhood, they are easy to find. "Just look for where things are a mess." Of course. *Muen* means lacking (*mu*) connection (*en*): having no one to tend to one's grave. But despite her own efforts to tidy her friend's grave and tend to his soul, his likely fate is to become a *muenbotoke* as well. As the priest tells her, it is up to the man's son to do the memorial rites (*kuyō*) and pay the annual maintenance fees at the temple. Because the son fails to do so, the father will soon become an abandoned soul. This means that his remains will eventually be moved from the family grave where he is marked by name and Buddhist name on a mortuary tablet to the grave for the disconnected, where his ashes will mingle with others and his identity will become both collective and unknown.

Just as she couldn't keep her friend tethered to life, Maia can't save him from abandonment in death, a fate that, as a single woman without children, could befall her as well. But whose responsibility is it to keep someone from dying or to memorialize them after death? This is an issue troubling many today at a time when Japanese are increasingly living and dying alone, and progressively dislodged from those ties—of family, work, locale—once expected to perform caregiving to both the living and the dead. One-third of all Japanese now live alone, one-fourth of the population is aged sixty-five and above (only 15 percent of whom live with a child), and the rates of both marriage and birth are declining. All the while, the rate of those dying annually has reached a historical high (making Japan a "mass death society"); the ranks of those irregularly employed have risen, which correlates with social isolation—men with regular jobs are twice as likely to marry as un(der)employed men; and the number of solitary nonemployed persons (SNEP) is rapidly on the rise. "Single-fication," as the sociologist Yamada Masahiro calls it,[2] is the new social fact of living and dying in twenty-first-century Japan. Reading this dystopically, Yamada sees in it a state of decaying sociality. Without recognition from others, or a set of relations to provide help and care in times of need, people are tasked with the self-responsibility (*jiko sekinin*) of managing their own existence. "Refugees" is what Yamada labels such isolates, bereft, he assumes, of family, society, and home.

But not everyone reacts to the new trend in single-fication with such dismay, finding in it new practices and modes of being with/out others that imply less the refugeeization of humanity than new possibilities for constituting social existence. Feminists such as Ueno Chizuko and Inoue Haruyo, for example, advocate "flexible" relations and services versus kin ties in managing end-of-life and mortuary arrangements, what Inoue calls turning to "midwives for death": the birthing of a new way of being at the time—and through the crucible—of death.[3]

This is the subject of my essay: how the ecology of attachment to others is rapidly changing in Japan, affecting and being affected by matters pertaining to death—both those involving mortuary arrangements increasingly made by the individual herself and those involving the risks posed by dying in/by solitude as in suicide or lonely death. Relational place is key here, for how one is placed vis-à-vis others has been critical for marking and grieving the dead. But just as the place of belonging is changing with the rise of single-fication, so is the place of the dead in the face of the shrinking role played by family and the family grave. Whether, for whom, and under what conditions these trends spell the emptying out of sociality (*muen shakai*) or, by contrast, new possibilities for arranging life and death with/out others are the questions I pursue. Looking at three different horizons aligned with different factors and characters in Japan's changing ecology of attachment and death, I consider both risks and opportunities in the shifts of relationality—shifts I see as revolving around place. What I argue in the end is that the social, particularly as normatively defined in the postwar era, is indeed undergoing transformation in twenty-first-century Japan. But it is not ending as much as morphing into something else: a sociality less dictated by durable ties of kinship and work in which new arrangements for belonging and new ways of being—both in and beyond mortality—is beginning to emerge. This article aims to track this emergent sociality in a state of becoming around matters of death.

One's Place in Death

One evening in August 2013 I arrange to meet two friends, middle-aged Japanese women, at a bar. One has just come from visiting the graves of an aunt and uncle buried in a Buddhist temple nearby. We are in Shinjuku, a high-rise district in Tokyo, and the woman is matter-of-fact when explaining how her relatives are buried. Because both were single, their remains could not be interred in a family plot where children perform the ritual of memorial. So they arranged instead for a new practice, started in the late 1980s but now spreading rapidly across Japan, of *eitaikuyō* or eternal memorial where ashes are interred in a collective room and temple officiants rather than family perform *kuyō* (memorial).

When I visit this temple myself the following summer, I am told that there are two kinds of relationship one can have with the temple and two different forms of burial. One is to be a parishioner (entailing a long-term and more costly commitment) and to be buried in a plot held by the family. The other is to become a member of the Relationship Association (*En no kai*), which doesn't require joining the temple or even being Buddhist, and paying a one-time membership fee of 800,000 yen ($8,000, about one-fifth the cost of a regular grave). For this one receives an interment ceremony, yearly memorial rites, a Buddhist name (*kaimyo*) engraved on a memorial plaque, one's living name etched on a grave marker, and storage of one's remains in an individual urn for thirty-two years, after which time they go to a communal ossuary. The brochure for Tōchōji lays out the logic of eternal memorial in postfamilial terms. "With *En no kai*, one has the opportunity to choose a new style of burial made so that all pray according to relations transcending those of blood. . . . Being disconnected (*muen*) [from family] doesn't signal the absence of relationality altogether but rather the possibility of being open to new kinds of connectedness."[4]

The day I visit Tōchōji it is pouring down rain, and the temple is unimposing despite commanding an entire city block. The only one signed up for that morning's information session, I am seated, served tea, and then introduced to Ms. Yamada, who takes me through the structure of the temple following the bullet points in its tony brochure. An hour later we go on the tour. A four-hundred-year-old Sōtō Zen Buddhist temple, Tōchōji has been renovated multiple times. With its stylish blend of traditional and modern, the premises are calm and well tended. As we pass by the areas holding the family plots, Ms. Yamada notes that descendants are necessary for burial here. But the emphasis—in both spatial layout and guided tour—is on eitaikuyō, the new system of belonging and burial that the former head priest Takizawa Kazuo started in 1996 as a strategy to keep the temple solvent in struggling times.[5]

Buddhist temples are downsizing and closing all over Japan as religion retreats ever further in the lives of a population that highly self-reports as unreligious and, in the face of Japan's economic decline since the early 1990s, is becoming less willing or able to pay large donations to temples for funerals and burials.[6] But rather than sell or lease some of its land, a tactic taken by other urban temples, Takizawa decided to tweak the principles of temple membership and its strategies for servicing death. Adopting the system of eternal memorial and hiring a management firm to help run the Relationship Association, Tōchōji gained eight thousand new members by 2004 and had sold all its ten thousand spots for eternal burial by 2008. Tōchōji has been given new life as a result of its new management of the dead.[7] But it is not economics that Ms. Yamada stresses in explaining the rationale of eitaikuyō. Rather, her account is sociological; it once was the extended family, then the nuclear family, and now the individual who buries the deceased. Somewhat unsettled, I ask, what comes next? But Ms. Yamada sees nothing but advantages in the direction things are going. Under the new system, there is more "freedom" in who can pay respects to the dead (not just family but also friends) and more egalitarianism in burial itself (every member here receives a Buddhist name for the deceased, and in a form undifferentiated by price).

According to Mark Rowe, the practice of eternal memorial promotes "limitless connections."[8] Rather than being limited to kin for burial and memorialization, or stranded as an "abandoned soul" when family is lacking, joining a burial association promises a different kind of relationality around death. This is indeed the language used in the Tōchōji brochure to advertise eitaikuyō: a form of connection that "opens up" even before one actually dies. Upon becoming a member of the Relationship Association, one can join a volunteer project, attend a retreat on Buddhism ending in a conferral ceremony for new members, and participate in a memorial held the first day of every month for the deceased. And, once dead, one is interred alongside fellow members in a space where everyone laterally (rather than vertically as with family vis-à-vis ancestors) belongs. The actual remains—ashes and bone fragments—are buried in urns two floors below the main premises where visitors are asked to burn incense first for the benefit of those who have no one to visit them. And on the main floor there are two spaces where the deceased are memorialized by name. In the Hall of a Thousand Hands, everyone has a memorial tablet (*ihai*) inscribed with their *kaimyo* (in red for those still alive). Living names go on black granite grave markers in one of three places. One is an idyllic water garden (*mizu no niwa*), where a monthly memorial is held when visitors light votive candles at dusk to pay their respect to the deceased—theirs and everyone else's.

With its practice of eternal memorial, Tōchōji offers Japanese a new place to go when dead. But, disagreeing with Rowe, I find the connections here not really "limitless" but dependent on an entrance fee and formed (only) with other members and temple staff. Rather than pure freedom, the appeal of eitaikuyō would seem to be one of security: securing a place to go and commercial mourners instead of family, one of many services burgeoning in the new market in end of life (*shūkatsu*) targeting the increasing demographics of the aging and single-fied in Japan today. Certainly, as I have learned from doing fieldwork on the subject since the summer of 2013, where to place the dead and the place death itself assumes in the currency of connectedness are troubling issues these days, and not easy to sort out, given shifting social and familial dynamics. Many people are single and don't "fit" the family grave even if there is one. For others, there is no family grave—this happened to a friend when her father died unexpectedly in his early sixties. He was the second son, in a system of primogeniture where traditionally only the first son is buried in the family grave. The family had not yet purchased a plot but then acquired one in great haste and at considerable expense.

For another woman, the fact that she has married and thus changed her maiden name, required by law, prevents her from entering her father's family plot (and her husband's family doesn't have one). Childless, she also has no one to perform memorial services, which by Buddhist custom should be done twice a year and on regular anniversaries of death for a period up to thirty-three years. But her worries extend to her parents as well: an aging mother who lives far away but close to her dead father's grave. Relocating her mother to care for her would mean abandoning the father in his grave left behind. All of this has become so troubling—to this woman, a political radical who claims no religious tendencies at all—that she has difficulty sleeping at night. When we visit a temple that practices eternal memorial close to where she lives in Niigata Prefecture (the Nichiren temple Kakuda Myōkōji), the priest tells her that "this is nothing to worry about" and that flexible arrangements—of connection, of memorial—can be made here. He should know—with only daughters and no grandsons, he faces the same problem of no place to go upon death and no one to take over the temple.

It was anticipating this situation that inspired Ogawa Eiji, the head priest of Myōkōji, to start the first system of eternal memorial in the country, in a collective memorial mound called Annonbyō. This was 1989, the same year he wrote what was a controversial article, "How to Avoid Dying without a Grave," in the Asahi weekly journal. Noting how the burial system had long been tied to the family and family graves at Buddhist temples, he advocated changing this in accordance with shifts in family and religious sentiment across the country. His position was that it should be acceptable to be buried outside family attachments, as an individual or communally.[9] While initially the article and Annonbyō generated much criticism, now it is the opposite, Ogawa tells us. People are constantly coming to Myōkōji for seminars and to seek out advice: both individuals struggling with the issue of where to go when they die (and not just those who are single or childless) and Buddhist practitioners keen to know how to diversify their religious practice. And in both cases, if inversely, there is also the issue of money: of individuals wanting to save on mortuary costs and of Buddhist practitioners wanting to build business. As Ogawa told me,

> the work Buddhist temples used to do is diminishing; the cremation business has decreased, and temples and graves are not as important as they once were. There used to be a system of primogeniture; in return for taking care of the elderly, the eldest son would receive property and his place in the grave. There was respect for the land that was tied to ancestors and also the temple. When people died, they thought they were reconnecting to ancestors, and this was comforting. But this ideology of death is fading today. We have entered an era when people no longer believe the temple is necessary. And while, during the bubble economy [1970s and 1980s], people spent a lot on funerals and graves, today that period is over, and people are now looking for ways to save money. More are doing just family funerals or direct funerals at the grave. And a communal burial space [eternal memorial] is one way to save money.[10]

As Ogawa concludes at the end of the two hours we spend with him, "I see the breakdown of the family system in Japan today as giving religion a new chance."

But according to Inoue Haruyo, the relationship goes the opposite way; it is the breakdown of the Buddhist burial system that is giving the family, and particularly women vis-à-vis family, a new chance. A feminist and nonfiction writer when she read his article in 1989, Inoue started collaborating with Ogawa. As she argued in her 1980 book advocating that women retain their maiden names upon marriage, Inoue has long felt that Japan's customary (and legal) system of succession (*keishō seido*) is discriminatory against women. When her mother died at age sixty-two, she was graveless; unable to enter the family plot of her father (because her married name was different), she could not enter the family plot of her husband either (because he was a second son and hadn't yet purchased his own family plot). The experience was horrible, Inoue wrote, making her keenly aware of how women, as daughters, become "relationless" (*muen ni naru*) under Japan's succession system, particularly at the time of death.[11] Having returned to school to study sociology, Inoue is now a professor and prominent figure in the emerging field around life and death in Japan. A leading advocate for the human rights of the dead, she is also a practitioner who started Ending Center, a citizen's group for treating death and postmortuary practices with respect. This was in 1989, and Ending Center has now evolved into a registered nonprofit organization (NPO) with burial grounds of its own.

Located on the outskirts of Tokyo within a beautiful Buddhist cemetery strewn with cherry trees,[12] Ending Center identifies itself by both practice and place: this is a graveyard for conducting funerals with cherry blossoms (*sakurasō*). With five different burial areas, all differently priced and designed (one where ashes go directly in the ground and all with the names of the deceased written discreetly on walls), Ending Center offers postmortem services in a natural setting without the need to depend on family. These are the two most common reasons for those who choose to be buried here, Inoue tells me the day I visit. And the two logics blur. The dead commune with nature in a burial ground where this and other forms of companionship take the place of or eliminate the need for family. As with those temples offering eternal memorial service, Ending Center provides both a place to go and a form of relationality after death. Here, though, because there is no direct affiliation with Buddhism, memorial (*kuyō*) is not part of the package. Instead, upon becoming a member (and paying for burial there), one is offered a different sort of connectedness. The dead are never alone here, the brochure points out, because one has a support network of flexible relations, including those provided by falling cherry blossoms and pets (coburial is acceptable).

Being "midwives" (*josanfu*) for death is how Inoue conceptualizes the work done by Ending Center, which helps individuals manage the end of life in their own way (*jibunrashi*) and form companionship for the future when dead.[13] This could be a "grave friend" (*hakatomo*), a word coined by Inoue for making friends with someone who will be buried nearby. When I attend a forum at Ending Center in the summer of 2016, members readily tell me they are "grave friends" with one another. A man tells me he has already attended one of the monthly get-togethers and looks forward to more. And a bubbly woman greets me by pointing to her nametag, where the number of her grave site is written next to her name: her place when dead has become part of her identity, and sociality, when still alive. Yet Ending Center promises not only the possibility of new forms of relationality around death but also the dissolution of older forms of relationality that bound one during life. According to Inoue, at least 10 percent of women seeking new burial practices are doing so to avoid being buried in their husband's family plot, still tied to mother-in-law and spouse. Inoue calls this "postdeath divorce."

The Place of Others in Life

The feminist Ueno Chizuko has written many books on being alone. Two have been best sellers, *Ohitorisama no rōgo* (*Aging Alone* [2007]) and *Otoko ohitorisama dō* (*The Path of a Gentleman Alone* [2009]), which are guidebooks of sorts for managing single life as one ages. Turning now to "dying single at home" (*zaitaku hitori shi*, the term she prefers to "lonely death")—the condition but also choice of an increasing number of aging Japanese, including herself—Ueno seeks viable ways to do this both within and beyond the medical profession. In the context of a new care insurance policy instituted in 2000 that facilitates, in her opinion, staying at home until death, Ueno describes resources for home health care in her 2015 books *Kea no karisumatachi* (*Care Charismatics*) and *Ohitorisama no saigo* (*End of Life for the Single Person*). Having been motivated to write these books to counter the discrimination she has faced as a single woman, Ueno is invested in making solitary existence more robust. One avenue is coming up with alternative networks beyond the family for managing life/death (having many good friends is a lot better than a bad marriage, she has quipped).

A highly respected scholar who taught anthropology at Tokyo University and remains a prolific author, Ueno is now retired and has started her own NPO, Women's Action Network. Living and dying alone can certainly bring misery, Ueno acknowledges. But in all the recent media attention given to such phenomena as lonely death, there is the recurring question of where is the family that she contests. The overriding assumption is that family is key to social security and connection, the premise, for example, in a series the Asahi newspaper ran on Japan's trend toward disconnectedness (titled "The Country of Lonely Belonging"). In her own contribution to the series, Ueno critically assesses the postwar Japanese family. Tied as it is to productivity and corporate capitalism, the family is expected to foster ties (*kizuna*) conducive to high output and competitive performance (for men at work, women at home, and children at school). In an argument that I have made myself,[14] this is a form of belonging that itself can produce loneliness and stress. In reproducing and incubating the pressures of society, family comes with its own set of risks. Considering the pitfalls of family formation, "What's so bad about being alone?" Ueno queries.[15]

In her life as well as her work, Ueno has consistently critiqued the marital norm in postwar Japan that accords social capital to the married and discounts childless singles (particularly women) as losers. Embracing feminist politics, she urges Japanese to find alternative socialities for sustaining existence and decries the inevitability of loneliness or estrangement for those without children or spouse. Her message—the liveliness of the Japanese single—is being given ever more attention by the press and the general public alongside the demographic expansion of the unmarried, childless, single households, and elderly in Japan. The role played, but increasingly evacuated, by family is certainly a cross-gender issue these days. But it is also gendered. Women are said to be better at communicating and making friends, which helps sustain them in living alone. And for men, whether or not one has a steady job seems as critical, if not more, than the presence of familial/social others in being at risk for isolation. This is the narrative I have been told repeatedly for why 80 percent of those who die isolated deaths are men, mainly unemployed. When a man lives to work (*ikigai*) and socializes almost exclusively with fellow workers, he loses his sense of belonging when retired or out of a job—as I was told by someone who cleans up the rooms of people who die all alone and are discovered sometimes weeks later. This is also the finding of labor historian Genda Yūji on the phenomenon of SNEP: solitary nonemployed persons (*koritsu mushoku*),[16] defined as unmarried, unemployed persons not connected to people outside family.[17]

According to government statistics, the number of SNEP younger than sixty was 2,559,000 in 2011, 63 percent of whom it identified as solitary. (This was based on those who answered that they had not done anything such as have a conversation with a person outside the family in the past two days.) Between 1996 and 2011 the total number of SNEP doubled, a symptom of what Genda considers to be the insecuritization of labor and life in Japan today, particularly for middle-aged men.[18] As shown in his earlier work on NEET (not in education, employment, or training), young people were hit hard by the collapse of the bubble economy in 1991 when a "lost generation" of youth couldn't find permanent jobs. But the category, officially defined as age eighteen to thirty-four, has now spread in what Genda terms a "NEET-ification" of older workers as construction companies closed down, manufacturing grew strong overseas, and the yen inflated in the late 1990s. Many middle-aged and older workers lost their jobs and couldn't find or didn't look for other employment. According to Genda, this is the demographic increasingly at risk for and prone to solitarization. And while more have family than not (of 1,623,000 SNEP in 2011, 80 percent lived with family), this does not necessarily shield them from isolation; two-thirds still report as solitary. SNEP are vulnerable to depression, suicide, and lonely death. They are also no longer exceptional. Genda ends his book on SNEP with guidelines for not falling prey to becoming SNEP: look for work of any kind, take up an activity or join a group, be motivated, and don't give up.[19]

The founder of hope studies (*kibōgaku*) at Tokyo University, Genda places much hope in place—finding a place (ideally at a job), attaching to something one can work at, being a part of a group larger than oneself. I find his study of SNEP sharp edged and important. But I also think what he is capturing—men who get isolated without an anchor to work—reflects a postwar vision of Japan as a growth economy fed by, and feeding, the productivity of core workers (mainly men) that is not only tremendously fraught but also increasingly unsustainable in what some call the postgrowth Japan of today. That a job itself, sometimes with the addition of marriage and children, does not necessarily produce social/psychic security is the insight of psychiatrist Saitō Tamaki in his article "Depression and Japan's Corporate Culture," cowritten with Jō Shigeyuki.[20] As he has noticed from his practice, a new form of depression has emerged over the past ten years. While difficult to figure out, it seems that those who are most prone to it have already become "social adults" (*shakaijin*) marked by permanent jobs, marriage, or both. Men in their thirties are particularly likely candidates who become depressed (leading sometimes to suicide) after losing a job or are simply struggling to remain competitive at the stage before they are due, in their forties, to advance to divisional or sectional head in the company.[21] For those trying to enter, or already inside, Japan's corporate culture the pressure to perform is intense, and this collides with the fact that the level of satisfaction with work and one's company is the lowest in Japan of all industrialized countries.

So even those who have the jobs that SNEP so sorely lack are at risk of depression, rates of which are rising among company workers, as they are in the population in general. And while Japan's high rate of suicide started to fall in 2012, the one contingent for whom this is not true and for whom suicide is continuing to rise are men in their thirties. Losing a job (even when this comes from quitting it oneself) is often what precipitates suicide, but so is never getting one in the first place for those a generation younger entering the job market in May. Suicides spike in the months of May and now June, and "disease of the heart" (*kokoro no byō*), as depression is euphemistically called in Japan, has taken hold around the long-term company job both for those excluded from it and for those stressed within just such a job.[22]

In the attention he pays to the relationship between depression and Japan's corporate culture, Saitō puts his finger on something else: a dark hole in the very idea of place itself as what confers identity and ties of belonging to others. It is not only that people are nervous about (not) getting regular jobs or (not) getting married and having children. These very pathways to adulthood are themselves contested or found to be precarious in their own right. A strange new form of depression, Saitō calls the latest disease of the heart among Japanese. And at risk is anyone—with or without job, living with family or all alone.[23] This would seem consistent with the kind of existential anxiety that seems to be springing up among Japanese youth, according to Usui Mafumi, a social psychologist at Niigata Seiryō University whom I interviewed about the online site for suicide prevention he started in 1997. In asking high school students he works with as counselor what they feel anxious (*fuan*) about, the third most common answer, after their abilities and future, is their very existence: Why am I alive? Why do I exist? Why was I born? Unsure of who they are and their place in the world, they find that existence itself makes little sense.

When I talk with Usui the summer of 2014, he reports being worried about Japanese teenagers today, whom he finds timid and withdrawn. In his assessment, they are growing up in a world where there are too few roadmaps for who or what to become, a situation fraught with social and existential risks for the young.

> In Japan, everyone wants to be ordinary—just to fit in with everyone else. If girls fail [at school], they can stay at home and help out. But boys have nothing else after failing at school or work; they become socially withdrawn (*hikikomori*). Japan has become a country where people lack self-confidence. It used to be that, even if someone was poor, they could have confidence and hope—as long as they didn't kill someone or do something grievously wrong. But we don't have that mind-set any more. Local relations (*chiikisei*) used to be strong. But now we have few bonds like this. People do want relations (*tsunagaru*) with one another, but no one knows how to communicate anymore.[24]

According to Usui, young Japanese have become "speechless" (*mugon*: *mu* for lacking, *gon* for speech, 無言). While everyone has a cell phone and is constantly twittering on social media, no one really talks, and especially not about those things that may be troubling them—an observation others have made about youth culture/sociality in Japan today, where the dynamics of belonging can be brutal and cutthroat.[25] The presence of others may be risky, even deadly, as in the cases of bullying that have led, in the extreme, to suicide. For some students, the easiest path is social exit or retreat, what Usui sees in a recent trend at his high school of fashion masks (*deta masuku*). Face masks are commonly worn in Japan when someone has a cough or cold to protect the spread of germs. But here they are worn when healthy, ensconcing the wearer in a *cordon solitaire*. It's not that these kids don't want relations with others, Usui says. Afraid of getting hurt, they wear the mask to feel better. Astute about the anxiety the very proximity to others can engender, Usui attributes the behavior of fashion masks to fear. But one could also read into these acts far more agency than he does. Engaging in a form of playful in(ter)vention, these "speechless" youth are learning how to survive in an ecology of changing relationality: behind a mask but in public nonetheless.

A Practice for Living

As a young man, Nemoto Jōtetsu was unruly and wild. He stayed out late listening to music, routinely got into fights, and studied philosophy at university but never graduated. Along the way, he worked at various jobs but took nothing too seriously. One day, more as a joke, his mother showed him a recruitment ad for Buddhist priests. But the son was intrigued, and, getting the job, he started working as an entry-level monk doing pet funerals. The job didn't require he be trained, but soon, wanting to learn more, Nemoto entered a Rinzai Zen monastery where the training is so grueling that most initiates don't make it through. Given that "a well-trained monk lives as though he were already dead,"[26] few remain in Japan today; Nemoto's monastery only has seven. The focus of the Rinzai Zen sect is individual enlightenment, what Nemoto practiced for four years inside the monastery. He then decided to leave to reacquaint himself with life outside. Taking a job at a fast food restaurant in Tokyo, he enjoyed the lightness of the work and the banter with customers and staff. Things were good. But his training hadn't been for this, he was told by his sect, who needed trained monks to become abbots of temples that were closing across the country.

A small Rinzai Zen temple in the rice fields of Seki city in Gifu Prefecture, Daizenji had lost its abbot and was on the verge of collapse when Nemoto agreed to step in. Built during the Heian period over a thousand years ago, Daizenji required major renovations to keep it alive. This was Nemoto's first order of business: raising the funds needed for the physical repairs. Once this was managed, reconstruction began, and today the temple is beautiful as a result. The day I visit in June 2014, Nemoto points out the pieces of roof sitting on the ground from the reconstruction. "They're three hundred years old," he says with a smile. As head priest of Daizenji, Nemoto has eighty-eight parishioners whom he tends to in all the usual ways: presiding over funerals, memorial services, and the everyday running of the temple. But Nemoto also engages in something else that extends, by tweaking, the Buddhist work of managing the dead: tending to the still living who are contemplating self-death (*jishi*, the word he prefers to suicide, *jisatsu*).

Having suffered the death of an uncle and two high school friends from suicide when younger, Nemoto had long been intrigued by the pain of humans that puts them in a vise between life and death. As he discovered that people easily opened up to him when working at the fast food restaurant, Nemoto started holding workshops on death and for *hikikomori* (socially withdrawn) at Daizenji. At the same time, he began a suicide website. Responding to everyone—which often migrated to phone calls and face-to-face encounters—Nemoto was endlessly engaged, 24–7. He also became exhausted from the emotional engagements of this constant work in near-death. Eventually getting sick, he was discovered to have blocked arteries and underwent four angioplasties over a two-year period. Posting about his illness, Nemoto was surprised at the cold reactions. No one seemed to care, absorbed as they were in their own issues. Disheartened, he considered giving up counseling. After giving it more thought, though, he decided to stick with his practice but to make some changes. One was demanding that, to communicate with him, everyone first meet him face-to-face.[27] This is why, in my case, too, I go to Daizenji.

Sitting in his temple, overlooking the rice fields, everything is quiet and still. Nemoto lingers over my questions, and answers are anything but quick. When I ask what he thinks accounts for the high rate of suicide, for example, he says, well, there's a long history of this in Japan. And today solitude (*kodokukan*) is widespread; many cannot connect or communicate with others or find a reason for living (*ikigai*). But in answer to whether certain contingents are more at risk, such as the un(der)-employed, Nemoto won't be pinned down. Yes, many young people who are irregularly employed are struggling, and because Japanese men tend to turn inward rather than express (or seek help for) their problems, this leads to stress and isolation. His emphasis, though, is on the fact that anyone can become lonely and depressed, even those with a family and a job. This is why Buddha, after all, left home and went into the world. Suffering is a fact of life, our existential condition, rather than a problem that is easily fixed. But without tending, the pain of living can fester out of control. Helping sufferers figure this out would seem to be Nemoto's mission.

Nemoto often speaks through example, of cases he has dealt with, like a woman in her thirties who had been suffering for years from an emotional disorder for which she had been taking regimen upon regimen of medication. Obsessed with her condition, she read everything on the subject and accumulated a library of information. Have you ever tried just letting it go? Nemoto asked her when she attended one of his workshops. After learning basic zazen, where one meditates by entering a space of nothingness (*mu*, 無), the woman tried it and found that something immediately shifted. Starting to get relief, she has continued the practice and now given up medication altogether.

Practice is important to Nemoto—practicing ways of being in the world that can keep us from self-death. Constantly experimenting with different methods and strategies for such a life practice, Nemoto tells me about one of his newest: a workshop called "playback theater." The third such one at Daizenji was held the weekend just before my visit, attended by thirty people, eighteen to forty-eight years of age, who signed up through a posting on social media. Over two days spent in a range of activities, including going to a nearby hot spring, special attention was paid to expression (*hyōgen*). This involved communication of various kinds: sharing stories of struggle and pain and "playing back" different ways of being in and around body and space—one's own and everyone else's. One such game they played involved a chain of motion: one person starts with a movement (such as a cartwheel) and then touches the next person, who does his or her own thing (like a headstand), who then touches the next person, triggering a round robin of touching/moving/morphing that spreads around the circle.

Being here, in the midst of others and as part of an event, feels good, Nemoto says. But once everyone leaves it is easy to slip back into depression and loneliness. Then staying in touch with people met during the workshop is important, as is maintaining something of the practice of life learned during the theater to prevent death held by the Buddhist priest at his Rinzai Zen temple among rice fields in Japan.

Conclusion

Much of what I have read and encountered in the field on the subjects I take up here—the rise of singular living, the shift away from a sociality based on long-term bonds, solitary death, and eternal memorialization—gets articulated, at some point, through the Japanese character 無 (*mu*, absence). There are the relationless souls (*muenbotoke*), Japan's derelational society (*muen shakai*), the solitary unemployed (*koritsu mushoku*), and the speechless youth (*mugon*) sheltered behind masks. And in the face of what is often taken to be a voiding of sociality now much talked about in Japan, there are models posed for countering the risks of solitarization, many of which involve forging new connections: volunteering or getting a less pressured job (as Genda suggests for SNEP and Saitō for the corporately depressed) and joining a temple with eternal memorial (to avoid ending up as a relationless soul upon death). Place is critical in this flux around connectivity, as I have tried to show in this article. Where one fits (or not) and what or who determines the fitting (or no longer does so) affect the dead as well as the living. And, in both cases, there is a lot of stress and struggle around place/lessness—an anxiety that also plagues the nation at a time when Japan faces a host of domestic problems, from an aging/declining population to postnuclear security, and its "miracle economy" of the postwar era seems forever a thing of the past.

But absence—of fitting in, of belonging—is not the only story of twenty-first-century Japan. Out of the very strain around the social grammar of existence are emerging alternatives in the organization of life with/out others. There are the initiatives of those like Ueno Chizuko and Genda Yūji working to destigmatize the socially single and to offer support for living and dying without family or job. But there is also the effort, more radical in its implications for sociality, to rethink the very attachment to attachment altogether, to imagine a lifestyle, or death style, that does not privilege belonging to long-term organizations or groups, with the attendant risks, for those without such ties, of feeling abandoned at death. This is how I view the initiatives of Nemoto Jōtetsu, who urges those he counsels to not rush too quickly to replace one set of (lost) connections with another but, rather, to linger over the placelessness of (a more solitary) existence and try to inhabit it (without turning to a fake mask or self-death). As in his playback theater, emphasis is placed more on being than belonging, on reorienting one's subjectivity rather than finding a new place for oneself in yet another group (which is the case when signing up for eternal memorial, a membership that excludes those too poor to pay), and on cultivating a different way of being through practice, which may include zazen: meditation by mindfully detaching from the world into the emptiness of *mu* 無. This is something Nemoto now teaches at yoga and Zen sessions offered in public parks—another step toward moving Buddhism into the realm of the living and beyond merely managing the dead, and one in which *mu* (disconnection) signals not social death, as does the *mu* in relationless souls/society/youth, but a practice of life less dependent on a notion of a fixed place, with its implications for dis/belonging.

When I did fieldwork in Japan between 2008 and 2011 on what I call precarity—the sense of insecurity around jobs, marriage, future, and the everyday that has percolated in the country since the start of Japan's postbubble decline in 1991—an expression I continually encountered was *ibasho ga nai*: not having a place where one feels comfortable or at home. It was as if the aspirational ideal of the high-growth era of owning one's home (my-homeism) had dissolved into its antithesis: the fear/feel of having no home at all (no-homeism), the breakdown of groundedness itself—the image captured by *muen shakai* (disconnected society). But today, as I finish writing this in 2016, the tenor of the times seems to have subtly moved on. Not that real precariousness and insecurity aren't still experienced by many Japanese in many different ways—this is indeed the case. But I hear less mention of *ibasho ga nai* and more interest in making new arrangements for both living and dying, as in doing so alone. This means devising new concepts of place and home, as with eternal memorial. But it also has prompted experimentation around the borders of place itself: to where, how, and with whom people are attached and see themselves as socially placed. Prompted, I argue, by single-fication and the attention now given to management of the dead increasingly as a single subject, place and one's attachments over time are becoming more open and less fixed to a durable, linear sense of commitment (as in ties to ancestors at the family grave).

Yoga and Zen in the park where different people participate at each event; the recent rise in share houses, where coresidents can be anyone and stay for varying lengths of time; graves that are not only the end point for the dead but also gathering spots for the living (as advertised by an NPO with a collective burial spot for single women); a company that sells pendants as "portable memorials" for the ashes of loved ones (including pets) that have been otherwise scattered at sea. As single-fication becomes the state of ever more Japanese, as surely it will, how single people engineer getting through life, including the end, and on whom or what they can count to both give and receive help will be key in the shape sociality assumes in future Japan. The point I have tried to make in this essay is that this sociality to come is already emergent today and can be seen in innovations given to dealing with—and learning from—the dead.

Notes

1. The price varies considerably depending on a number of factors, such as whether or not, and what level, the deceased is given a *kaimyo* (Buddhist name) by a priest, which according to a survey by the National Funeral Association of Japan averaged 498,000 yen ($4,140) in 1999. Danely, *Aging and Loss.*

2. Yamada, *Kazoku nanmin.*

3. Ueno, *Kea no karisumatachi*; Inoue, *Sakurasō.*

4. Tōchōji, *En no kai boen*, 2.

5. Rowe, *Bonds of the Dead.*

6. Reader, *Religion in Contemporary Japan*; Danely, *Aging and Loss*; Traphagan, *The Practice of Concern*; Kitano, *Nature's Embrace.*

7. Rowe, *Bonds of the Dead.*

8. Ibid., 112.

9. Kitano, *Nature's Embrace.*

10. Ogawa Eiji, interview by the author at Myōkōji in Niigata, 12 June 2014. Unless otherwise noted, all translations are my own.

11. Inoue, *Sakurasō*, 12.

12. While Machida Izumi Jōen is a Buddhist cemetery, Ending Center itself is not affiliated.

13. Inoue, *Sakurasō.*

14. Allison, *Precarious Japan.*

15. Ueno, "Otoko yo, sotsujiki ni yowasa wo mitomeryō," 16.

16. Genda, *Koritsu mushoku SNEP.*

17. Because so many unemployed are married women who, not working, are supported on a husband's salary, the category "unmarried, unemployed" is intended to capture those without either jobs or spouses.

18. The decline (and delay) of both marriage and childbirth also correlates with Japan's economic downturn. Men with regular jobs are twice as likely to marry and have children as those un(der)employed, and women say they will not marry anyone without a steady job (and are remaining single and childless in greater numbers than ever before in large part, if not exclusively, because of economic insecurity). Genda, *Koritsu mushoku SNEP*; Yamada, *Kazoku nanmin.*

19. Genda, *Koritsu mushoku SNEP.*

20. Saitō and Shigeyuki, "Nihon no kigyōbunka to 'kokoro no byō.'"

21. This is a point also made by Tanaka Toshiyuki, sociologist and founder of new "male studies," in *Otokoga tsuraiyo.*

22. Saitō and Shigeyuki, "Nihon no kigyōbunka to 'kokoro no byō.'"

23. Ibid.

24. Usui Mafumi, interview by the author in Niigata City, 12 June 2014.

25. Allison, *Precarious Japan.*

26. MacFarquhar, "Last Call," 60.

27. Ibid.

References

Allison, Anne. 2013. *Precarious Japan.* Durham, NC: Duke University Press.

Danely, Jason. 2014. *Aging and Loss: Mourning and Maturity in Contemporary Japan.* New Brunswick, NJ: Rutgers University Press.

Genda, Yūji. 2013. *Koritsu mushoku* SNEP (*The Solitary Unemployed SNEP*). Tokyo: Nihon Keizai Shinbun Shuppansha.

Inoue, Haruyo. 2012. *Sakurasō: Sakura no shita de nemuritai* (*Cherry Blossom Funerals: I Want to Sleep under a Cherry Tree*). Tokyo: Sanseido.

Kitano, Satsuki. 2010. *Nature's Embrace: Japan's Aging Urbanities and New Death Rites.* Honolulu: University of Hawai'i Press.

MacFarquhar, Larissa. 2013. "Last Call: A Buddhist Monk Confronts Japan's Suicide Culture." *New Yorker*, 24 June, 56–63.

Reader, Ian. 1991. *Religion in Contemporary Japan.* Honolulu: University of Hawai'i Press.

Rowe, Mark. 2011. *Bonds of the Dead: Temples, Burial, and the Transformation of Japanese Buddhism.* Chicago: University of Chicago Press.

Saitō, Tamaki, and Jō Shigeyuki. 2014. "Nihon no kigyōbunka to 'kokoro no byō'" ("Depression and Japan's Corporate Culture"). *Ushio*, June, 150–57.

Tanaka, Toshiyuki. 2015. *Otokoga tsuraiyo: Zetsubō no jidai no kibō no danseigaku* (*It's Hard Being a Man: The Hope of Male Studies in an Era of Despair*). Tokyo: Kadokawa.

Tōchōji. 2014. *En no kai boen: Mizu no niwa* (*Cemetery Garden for the Relational Association: Water Garden*). Tokyo: Tōchōji.

Traphagan, John W. 2004. *The Practice of Concern: Ritual, Well-Being, and Aging in Rural Japan.* Durham, NC: Carolina Academic Press.

Ueno, Chizuko. 2012. "Otoko yo, sotsujiki ni yowasa wo mitomeryō" ("Men, Let's Recognize Their Weakness at Graduation"). In *Kozoku no kuni: Hitoriga tsuna-*

garu jidai he (*Solitary Tribe Country: Toward Single People Making Relationships*), 115–18. Tokyo: Asahi Shinbun Shuppan.
Ueno, Chizuko. 2015. *Kea no karisumatachi: Mitori wo sasaeru purofuesshyonaru* (*Care Charismatics: Professionals Who Support Nursing*). Tokyo: Akishobo.
Yamada, Masahiro. 2014. *Kazoku nanmin* (*Refugees from the Family*). Tokyo: Asahi Shinbun Shuppan.

Something, Everything, Nothing; or, Cows, Dogs, and Maggots

Naisargi N. Dave

In Rajasthan in 2013, I met a woman named Timmie Kumar, whom other animal activists across India love and respect for her work with a renowned shelter in Jaipur. The first time we met we connected instantly and had a long and meandering talk. Her commitment to her work is evident, but so too is its toll. "I have to stop now," she said. "I just have to. I didn't want to do nothing. But somehow nothing became everything, and I started to drown."

This article tries to locate the missing *something* that would have prevented her from drowning or, to cast the problem more widely, the missing something that enables any alternative social project to persevere. I argue that we will find that missing something buried in and by the tyranny of consistency, which demands that any ethics in an oppositional or oblique relationship to the way things are (we might call this an ethic of the otherwise) account for its apparent inconsistencies or contradictions. Under the tyranny of consistency—or what I'll call contradiction thinking—an act such as rescuing a pig raises the question of why Timmie does not rescue every pig, every animal, or, for that matter, how she could ever swat at a mosquito. Contradiction thinking sees in such inconsistencies ethically nullifying contradictions but fails to acknowledge two uncomfortable truths about itself: that such equivalencies are merely convenient and rote, reflecting not moral truth but a language ideology in which a pig, all animals, and a mosquito are even thinkable together; and that the normative man, when acting normatively, is rarely called upon to account for his contradictions (in fact, we can probably define the normative as that which is allowed to be and remain in contradiction without existential consequence). The difference for Timmie is that her inconsistencies mat-

DOI 10.1215/01642472-3727984 © 2017 Duke University Press

ter because her actions are, or are felt to be, a critical commentary on the values of the world as it is.

The tyranny of consistency has one primary and deceptively ordinary function: to exhaust—and I mean, literally, to make people tired so that they give up. It is a primary modality of what Peter Sloterdijk calls cynical reason, the combatant consciousness of enlightened modernity in which reason is put to the service of "maintaining us without extending us."[1] Its antagonist, as Elizabeth Povinelli might put it, is the perseverance of the ethically otherwise.[2] The tyranny of consistency steals the something we need by collapsing something with everything, so that all we are left with (because everything is impossible) is nothing, which is both impossible and extinguishing. Importantly, the tyranny of consistency is a demand not only from outside but also from within; the ethically otherwise, after all, still belongs to, and emerges from, the world as it is. The ethically otherwise not only finds itself responding to tyrannical calls for consistency but also is a closet tyrant itself, always demanding more, asking, "if this thing, then why not that thing also—yes, yes, you're right," until eventually all the world can potentially make a moral claim on it. The tyranny of consistency succeeds in exhausting the ethically otherwise through this descent into obligation: Timmie drowns into infinite responsibility.

If the tyranny of consistency steals the something we need for our social projects to persevere, what are our options? One, of course, is to give up the otherwise, to be finally exhausted. This might take the form of drowning and disappearing, or it might take the form of folding quietly back into the world as it is. The latter would be a relief, for the world as it is, the normative, is not subject to the tyranny of consistency (it just speaks to its otherwise *as* the tyranny of consistency). But what about those who want neither to drown nor to speak to the world as tyrants, folded back into the world as it is? They, I argue, generate the something through an immanent ethics: the ethics of the otherwise in perseverance. Immanent ethics is the creative, lived response to the tyrannical formula, "if something, then everything, and if not, then nothing." Immanent ethics makes the something habitable. This is a dangerous way of putting it, so let me be clear: this is different from the liberal ethos of "well, something is better than nothing, right?" The latter still sees the something normatively, that is, in a relationship of potential consistency with everything or nothing, as if everything and nothing are viable options at all. Immanent ethics makes the something habitable all by itself, a durative present in which everything and nothing are not alternatives to it but are one and the same within it: every something is everything (because in this moment it is all that matters), and every something is nothing (because it needn't be related, tyrannically, to anything else).[3]

This might all sound abstract, but it is the lesson I learned from doing ethnography, from being with people who live, or seek, an ethically otherwise—and struggle with, or sometimes simply shrug at, the tyranny of consistency. Immanent ethics exists, but it is necessarily vulnerable: to interrogation, to exhaustion. And so in this article I show how it is sought, how it is foiled, and, at times, how it perseveres.

Cows

Retired Brigadier General Chauhan is a slight man with a pleasant face, a mole on his left jaw, and a thick, white handlebar moustache. He is usually in a cap, eyeglasses, corduroy pants, and white sneakers, the soles packed with manure and grass. Chauhan is the director of a gaushala, or cow shelter, outside New Delhi. The road leading to Chauhan's gaushala is potholed and rough, but once you turn into it, the universe changes. A large gate opens automatically onto a paved path, and everything inside is freshly painted in greens and reds and whites. Devotional music plays over the loudspeakers. Thirteen hundred cows lived there when I was visiting in February 2013. They are fed under sheds named after rivers, with deep troughs that are cleaned daily, and the animals are fed a healthy mixture of green fodder, jaggery, and mineral supplement. They drop big mounds of dung, or *gobar*, as they go, fifteen tons a day in all, which the gaushala sells as its main source of revenue. The rest of its money comes from a foundation called the Vishnu Charitable Trust (VCT). Groups like the VCT run gaushalas, ostensibly, to save cows from lives of hardship. Sometimes they will take in cows abandoned by farmers after going dry, made now to wander the streets eating plastic bags and garbage. Many have been injured by cars. Sometimes these are rescues from animal transport vehicles, which carry cows from dairy farms to states like Kerala or West Bengal where cow slaughter is legal. The people who run groups like VCT—usually Hindus with conservative if not fundamentalist politics—are the same ones who demand antislaughter legislation in their own states, which then actually ensures that their dairy cows will not be slaughtered nearby but will be transported thousands of kilometers, in terrible conditions, to their death. And these gaushalas themselves are often big business, functioning as dairies and makeshift breeding centers. Chauhan used to sell milk from his gaushala, too, but after being relentlessly persuaded by a vegan activist friend of ours, he came to see it as exploitation.

I was there early one morning, before Chauhan arrived, and I stood under the bright blue sky, looking out over the cows. They had had their morning meal and were in their outdoor enclosures, dropping gobar or licking one another, swatting their tails about. Chauhan arrived and suggested we take a turn around the grounds. He had been giving me lessons all week on his favorite breeds, intermittently quizzing me on their characteristics. I guessed a Gir correctly, with a prominent hump, high forehead, and foot-long ears that lope downward. He spied his favorite cow, Kamadhenu, and ran toward her, asking me over and over again as he held her face in his hands, isn't she beautiful? I didn't think she was all that, personally, but what do I know? She had golden horns, a pink tongue, and golden hair at the tip of her tail. He urged me to whisper a wish in her ear, which I did; he beamed. Chauhan wrapped his entire body around Kamadhenu, kissing her face, stroking her dewlap, petting the length of her. I have never seen a man so happy. He told me that he gets to be a child again when he's with his cows. Well, first he said he *relives* childhood, but he corrected himself: he gets to *be* a child. He lived on a farm growing up, and they had chickens, cows, and dogs, but it was the cows he always loved best, he told me. He started to eat like them: on his hands and knees, eating peas and carrots from the ground with his tongue. His mother was mortified (are you insane? she asked him), but he kept on, on all fours. He was on all fours now, in fact, rolling around in a full embrace with a beautiful, brown purebred Sahival whose neck was heavy with *malas*, the bright blue one signifying "Do not sell to anyone!" Chauhan took a brush from his pocket (heart patients come to the gaushala regularly to brush the cows; it is said to reduce their blood pressure). The Sahival's flank was caked with dung and mud as Chauhan brushed her, and then he put his finger between the bristles, plucked out some muck, and put that finger in his mouth. I looked at him inquisitively: what the hell? "You see!" he said. "The cow is your mother! She blesses you. She can never hurt you!" Here was a native, religio-scientific theory about the impossibility of maternal-fetal conflict, a lover boy's conception of the oneness of things, a virtuosic Harawayan performance of becoming with.

Later, sitting in his office, I think he felt I was being left out of his multispecies orgy. Would I like to drink some *gau mutra*, he asked? I said I would if he wanted me to. Casually, so that I wouldn't be alarmed by his excitement, he asked his assistant to send a woman out to the sheds to follow a cow around with a bucket and get me some pee to drink. We returned to talking, and then one of his thirty-three Nepali employees, an athletic-looking woman in a sari (whom, like the cows, Chauhan insists on calling Mother), walked in with a stainless steel cup. Chauhan asked her to pour the urine into a glass so that I could admire it properly. He drank first to show me that it's okay, and he drank it like it was Gatorade, or beer. He wiped his moustache with his sleeve and smacked his lips.

My turn. Not too bad, I said to Chauhan. I made a face, though, through which I tried to smile, while I took a bottle of water out from my bag and drank. I put it back, attempted another smile. He was delighted.

Brave girl! he said, several times: brave girl! "You are now an honorary—honorary *and honorable*—member of this gaushala! So many people have come here, devotees, *bhakts*, politicians, but until now nobody has tasted the gau mutra. 'I will vomit sir, please!' they say. 'Don't ask me!' But you," he said, "no dramatics, only action!"

As he went on, our mutual friend, Arpan, arrived, the vegan activist and convener of India's federation of animal protection organizations, FIAPO, the one who had convinced this milk-loving man to stop selling the stuff. Amazing girl! Chauhan shouted. What do you want with her, you devil? Arpan said he was taking me to lunch at his mother's house and apologized for not having prepared anything special. I just want something without pee in it, I told him. As we walked to Arpan's car, Chauhan chastised him for being so buttoned up, so utterly without affect. "You've taken this meditation business too far," he scolded Arpan. "You were already halfway mad, and when you get all the way mad you will have reached nirvana!" Arpan, Chauhan said, turning to me, won't brush cows or whisper wishes in their ears or drink the gau mutra because he doesn't believe in loving particular animals. That's right, Arpan said: cow, pig, dog, rat, Naisargi—they're all exactly the same to me.[4]

A dog is a rat is a pig is a Naisargi. Is this Arpan's closet tyrant, demanding from Chauhan utter consistency as the price he must pay for loving queerly, being otherwise, for adoring cows like a carefree kid on a farm? Because, really, why should Chauhan's love for cows mean anything for his relationship to rats, pigs, or me? Part of the problem for Arpan is in fact Chauhan's love, his excessive affect. Love is inconsistent and aberrant. That is its very point. As I argue elsewhere, love is the placeholder, the justification, for ethical inconsistency in the world as it is (moral abeyance or exception in the name of the one/s we love).[5] But the ethically otherwise does not have the luxury of aberration and exception, subject as it is—from within and without—to the tyranny of consistency. Arpan's turn away from an ethics laden with affect is a turn away from inconsistency, supposedly resolved by the tempered logic of radical equivalence (or radical consistency).[6] Here the tyranny of consistency would reach its goal, total exhaustion, for how could Arpan actually treat every rat, pig, dog, and human the same without driving himself mad with infinite obligation?

But Arpan didn't go mad; he didn't ultimately drown. That means either he gave up the otherwise, unable to do everything, or what looks like radical equivalency might take another form: an immanent ethics of the durative present. Here, "a dog is a rat is a pig is a Naisargi" does not mean that a dog is *the same as* a Naisargi, always and consistently, and therefore what is done for a human woman must also be done for every dog. It simply means that every act is its own something, ethically habitable all by itself, refusing the tyranny of consistency either in what I may not care for or in what I must. Read this way, the *is* in the phrase "a dog is a rat is pig is a Naisargi" is not the *is* of ontology but, instead, a chemical dissolution. I act not because you are that thing and I am this thing, or because our fates are bound up together, but because what else could be done in this moment?[7]

Dogs and Maggots

Cows are symbolically dense animals in India, sites of attachment for all sorts of fantasies about maternal love, communal encroachment, and the stability of a Brahminical order.[8] They are thus emotively rich. So too, for different reasons, are dogs. The summer of 2012 was my summer of dogs, and I spent most of it with a group called Welfare for Stray Dogs (WSD). WSD was founded in 1985 by a group of Jains concerned about mass municipal killings of stray dogs, in which animals were rounded up, thrown in a kennel with a thin layer of water, and electrocuted en masse. WSD began as a modest shelter in the heart of one of Bombay's largest slums, near Mahalaxmi station and Dhobi Ghat. That shelter is still there, modest but now thriving. And the Bombay (now Mumbai) municipality no longer culls dogs and then counts tails; now, they count surgically removed ovaries and testicles, accumulated in buckets, to register how many dogs the shelter has sterilized and sent peaceably back to the streets. Since 2002 it has been illegal for the city to kill strays; the new mode of population control is sterilization.

One of the people responsible for this cultural shift is Abodh Aras. Abodh is slim, with light black hair and striking gray-green eyes. Abodh is the CEO of WSD, and he claims to run it like the MBA that he is—methodical, routinized, and relying on consistent principles to save animals rather than the vagaries of the heart. He came to WSD as a teenager, after a healthy neighborhood puppy he had taken to a shelter was dead by morning due to rampant disease in the overcrowded space. He had given in to an impulse he now likens to hoarding: taking an animal off the streets to assuage his human guilt, collecting animals as living evidence of his own inability to accept injustice. Something else had to die for Abodh to perform his humanity.

Of course, it was that same humanity that he drew on to invent a program of street-based first aid. Abodh transformed WSD's shelter into one strictly for sterilization recovery and extreme cases of injury or illness that cannot be treated on the street. As for all the other maimed, half-blind, and maggot-ridden creatures, WSD makes a list based on calls to their helpline and then sends fieldworkers to find each one, treating them on their pavement dwellings to the best of their ability. Abodh started out as one of these fieldworkers, but now that he's CEO he spends most of his time in office clothes—except on Sunday.

It is widely known among the English newspaper–reading public in the city that at 9:30 every Sunday morning volunteers meet outside of Eros Cinema near Churchgate station to then make their way around the island city administering rudimentary treatment to wounded animals. Often the first one there, I would watch Abodh pull up in his maroon jalopy, wearing his yellow volunteer T-shirt and baggy blue jeans stained with an ointment called Himax that looks like caked blood. It would take him ten minutes to walk from the curb to where I was standing as the very smell of him brought dogs out from under cars and bus shelters and pedestrian subways and who knows where else, loping over to be handled and loved. We would eventually branch off in small groups, each with a smelly duffel bag full of instruments and applications and stained cotton balls, and with a list of animals that needed tending to. This particular morning I went off with Abodh and a young woman named Sumathi.

Our first animal was listed as simply "Dog. Oval maidan." So we walked over to the oval maidan and the tea seller, or *chai-wallah*, where the morning air smelled like cardamom and hot, sticky sweetness. The chai-wallah and his friends, upon seeing Abodh, immediately stood up and showed us a dog lying on the sidewalk. Abodh put his hands on the dog and knelt beside him as a friendly crowd of workers and loafers gathered around, all men and one boy in a soccer jersey. How old is the dog, Abodh asked the boy; 127, he answered, eyebrows furrowed. Abodh laughed, and one of the men playfully smacked the boy on his head. The dog seemed fine enough for a street dog until Abodh turned him over and lifted his head slightly. There, on his neck, was a red, festering wound that I could smell from where I was standing. Abodh called me in closer and pointed out a huge fluorescent green maggot wiggling around just under the pus and with a pair of tweezers picked it out and placed it in a cotton ball that Sumathi held out for him, which she then closed upon the fattened vermin firmly, killing it. (Later, when rolling down his car window to let a bug out, Abodh said, confessing to his inconsistencies: "The only things I don't mind killing are fleas and maggots.") Abodh placed some medicine on the wound—his hands still bare—and then a spray called Topicure, then Nebasulf powder, and finally, with his fingers, dabbed gobs of Himax over and just inside the wound. The crowd was rapt, and the chai-wallah shouted at them, get to work, there's nothing to see here, get to work! Everyone ignored him. It was clear that the chai-wallah liked the dog, too.

The animal now tended to, a different ritual began. Abodh stood up and looked at his hands. "Zara haath dhona hai?" (Could I wash my hands?), he asked nobody in particular. The chai-wallah gestured to another man with his chin, and the man rushed over to a rusty spigot, filled a tumbler with water, and picked up a creviced wafer of soap. Abodh held his hands out, and the man poured water slowly over them, placing the soap between Abodh's hands, pausing as Abodh cleaned quickly under his fingernails, and then rinsed Abodh's hands, the spent water spreading between them. The man, slightly bent over, stood up, taking the soap from Abodh's hands, and in this moment, something transpired between them that, though not quite visible, was still palpable. This unarticulated ritual occurred virtually every time Abodh treated an animal, an animal that despite its abjecting qualifier, *street*, was lodged in the hearts of the men and women who shared the street with him. That moment was always thick, the circuits of touch and intimacy mediated by the animal forging bonds of continuity between men of otherwise dissimilar worlds. These are indeed enduring bonds, fat with futurity. There are streets Abodh has trouble walking along because the hawkers and dwellers rush out to meet him, still insisting with smiles and back slaps on giving gifts for his healings of animals past. He refuses everything but touch.

Dipesh, however, moves through the world largely unhindered. Dipesh is one of WSD's fieldworkers. Six days a week he covers the city, from South Bombay to Matunga, by foot, bus, and train. I have seen him heal goats and donkeys, hens and crows, cats, cows, rats, and dogs. Dipesh is in his late twenties, but you wouldn't know it. His hair is thinning; he has tough, dark skin and a strong, thick body. He is big and strapping but Chaplinesque somehow, probably because of the torn and frayed pack on his back and another bag on his shoulder, the handles of which are crusted with years of bodily detritus, human and animal. He wears the same pair of light gray pants every day, with the same peach button-down shirt and thin black shoes with holes in them. He walks fast, despite the heavy bags, and is often on his cell phone, consulting with Abodh or the help line volunteer. He doesn't stop to eat or drink but has chai in the morning and a meal at 10:30 at night when he goes back to the chawl he shares with his parents. Dipesh is unmarried, but he has two siblings, both of whom have families of their own. I asked him once why he hadn't married. "Aa badha maate," he said, sweeping his arm as if to include all the invisible animals of the city. To have time for them, he continued in Gujarati, "*main life cycle finish nathi karyu*" (I haven't become husband and father).

Dipesh was whistling and chatting with me as we walked one day and suddenly turned and kneeled down near a motor scooter, out from under which he pulled an old, horrid-looking dog, with a tail like a thick, tapered rope and huge patches of fur missing, all pink and scaly like an armadillo. Still whistling, he pulled a string from the pocket of his pants and casually tied her snout and carried her into the partial shade of an apartment building. With his free hand, Dipesh grabbed a discarded newspaper, which he placed under the dog's butt. He lifted the animal's tail and applied medicine inside her anus with a dropper. Maggots emerged in the dozens, wriggling and wiggling, and Dipesh took his tweezers, entered the dog's ass, and pulled out dozens more, placing them methodically on the newspaper, by which time they had all stopped moving. When he finished the job, Dipesh applied talcum powder and an anti-infection cream and unmuzzled her. As Dipesh wadded up the newspaper, looking for a place to dispose of it, the dog walked unsteadily into the street and promptly took what looked like a very uncomfortable shit as cars and motor scooters dodged her. As a car nearly hit her, I screamed, and Dipesh turned to see. He waved his hand dismissively: she's old, he said.

I want to think about what this means—what it means to kneel bareheaded in the heat of the midday sun, pulling maggots deep from the ass of an unknown animal one by one, naked hands on its armadillo skin, whistling a tune to soothe her trembling body. And then, when you let her go, and she walks headlong into her own death, you shrug and say, "She's old." This is immanent ethics. This is love without a future, love that has no interest in bonds of continuity between man and man, man and animal, man and woman, something and everything. This is love that does not endure—for what is it to endure when there is no future—but simply *is*, the radical nowness of being this and becoming nothing and therefore everything, like the dog who suffers now so it is now that he will care for her, not for later and not for us, like Dipesh, whose life cycle is stopped, not suspended, not completed, not precarious, but stopped right here, a living death that enables life because of the presence of death in its every instant.

I want to say that Dipesh is an animal and his ethics are animal, too.[9] And having said it, I would *insist* that Dipesh is an animal, for what would it mean to deny it, to take it back? Wouldn't it mean to assert the abyss that separates human from animal, the same abyss between what counts as man and what does not that constitutes the chasm in which the boy in a soccer jersey lives under a tarp sharing his food with a maggot-ridden dog in a teeming, filthy city marred by a gulf between the rich and the destitute, wracked by decades of colonial rule and decades of government corruption such that when it rains whole streets cave in, and whole people die (forget the animals), and those who live, like Dipesh's father, are treated like capital and take to drink and stay that way such that his son has no choice but to give everything he has left to keep his mother and father alive? Isn't that what it would mean to say no, Dipesh is not an animal; he, like me, and unlike that, is a man?

"Everything I have," he said to me, "is for my family. But everything I *am* is this." Everything he is, is this, acting as this, not under humanity's signs of duty, pity, or compassion. Like Abodh, he does not say with sentimentality, "Poor dog, I will help him," and he does not cry or take the dog home, regardless of the horror before him. But unlike for Abodh, the animal mediates little but Dipesh's own animal sociality, a thick sociality to be sure, like the dogs on the streets who know companionship and bonhomie, but a thick sociality that exists always against a radical solitude—not the radical solitude of the molar subject of metaphysical humanism but the radical rhizomatic solitude that understands that love is an injustice because when we love it is only the one or ones who are special to us that we save.[10]

That is precisely what is important to me about Dipesh: he does not act in order to save. He does not act within what Didier Fassin has called "humanitarian reason," a kind of action that privileges affect ("this poor dog!") over structural inequality and injustice.[11] But neither does Dipesh reject the affective in favor of the reasonable (for the reasonable thing to do would have been to save the dog's life, after spending all that time on her). As Fassin himself points out, the critique of humanitarian reason, while necessary, veers too often into a blindness toward feeling, cynically conflating all suffering and its recognition with the cultural and governmental complexes (to wit, humanitarianism) that thrive upon them. What starts out as a critique becomes its own false truth: that suffering is but a construct, and those who traffic in it are agents of a neoliberal form of governance. Animal rights activism is often seen in just this way, and while it certainly deserves to be subject to a critique of humanitarian reason,[12] not all ethical engagements with animals can be dismissed as examples of it. What I seek to be open to, with Dipesh's story, are ethical instantiations that have little regard for the hallmarks of humanitarian reason: redemption and salvation, community and solidarity, humanity and its evidence, difference and equivalence, consistency and identity.[13]

But always, we come back to the problem of consistency. As I read it, Dipesh was making the *something* habitable, all by itself: this dog, those maggots, this moment, regardless of the death that hounds it. But when I tell this story, I am usually asked about the maggots: what does it mean that Dipesh killed them? How ethical is he, really, if he cares about dogs but kills maggots? "Account," the question demands, "for how the something is related to the everything."

I could simply dismiss this as the tyranny of consistency (which it is), but given that the question is usually posed to me from within, and in the spirit of, an ethically otherwise (we closet tyrants), I want to take seriously the point the question presents. The maggots: Aren't they a limit case? Don't they show us that we are doomed to make difference? That we are doomed to love and therefore to violence? That we are trapped in the humanist logic of this and that? Let me start by saying, yes, fine: the maggots are the limit case. Dipesh is not after all an animal: he is a man, a man like any other man who loves some things and not others, and loves those things that reflect back to him his own humanity—not immanently, but consistently. He is a man like any other man whose world is divided into animals promising and unpromising: the ones capable of having names and faces; the ones, like the maggots in the nameless but still promising dog's ass, that are not. The maggots are a limit case, too, in that they show us that ethics extinguish.[14] Ethics take an undifferentiated thing—a dog with maggots—and turn it into differentiated things: dogs, maggots. In turning an undifferentiated thing into differentiated things we create a choice, in which one of those things is extinguished (that is ethics). It is to say, in this case, to the wriggling maggot, fat with another's life (but it is not necessarily another's life; it is perfectly possible to see them as belonging to the same life, as mutually enfleshed), that I see you want to live, but I choose *this* animal, the one that promises.

Okay. Then what is it like *not* to choose? To *consistently* refuse choice?

Cows and Maggots, and Then a Dog

I was in Hyderabad in April and May 2013, living in the India office of Humane Society International. My host was a man named Jayasimha, thirty-two years of age, with a wife and baby son. He is brilliant and driven—admittedly obsessed with reducing animal suffering. He has a simple formula that guides his action: for every hour or dollar spent, how many animals can be saved? He will not save a dog if in the same amount of time or for the same amount of money he can save a chicken because that dog he has saved will, over the course of his life, eat a hundred chickens. It's pretty simple: a dog is a rat is a chicken. I don't know if this is just how he is or if he has learned to work hard at it, but he has no time for sentiment. There are two stories about him that I love to tell. I had brought two rather randomly chosen gifts for his son, whom I had never met: a stuffed dog and a wooden rattle. Jayasimha's desk was across the office from mine, and I looked up from my computer to see him playing with the toys himself, to show an employee how one might "humanely slaughter" a dog by "stunning it" in the head with the rattle and then using a letter opener to demonstrate how to slit its throat and skin it once it has been hung upside down. He caught me staring at him, my mouth open, and he blushed and put the toys away. The second story also involves his baby, whom we had taken to a restaurant with us and was crying inconsolably. We all cooed and bounced around with him to no avail until Jayasimha came in. "This is what I did when he was in the womb," he said, taking his child, and began reciting to him from memory full passages from *Fast Food Nation* and statistics about factory farming. The baby, of course, in the embrace of familiarity, fell peacefully asleep.

He picked me up from the airport the day I arrived and took me for lunch at the Secunderabad Club, where we made plans for things I should do and see. He was especially eager to take me to a three-story gaushala run by a wealthy Jain, a two-minute drive from where we were, in the heart of the city. Jayasimha came here often, always trying to find a way to shut the place down. He once told the director that there wouldn't be so many suffering cows in the world if he and his friends became vegan; he was escorted out of the gaushala for this unsolicited advice. Jayasimha primed me to be shocked by the place, and I was somewhat: this was no gaushala at all; it was a parking garage. Several vegetable vendors had set up shop near the entrance, selling food to people who would feed it to the bovine inmates above, earning divine favor. We walked up the ramp behind a suited man who was barking orders at a man who was, with difficulty, pushing a cart with grass the suited man had bought to feed to the cows. I had, frankly, seen worse places, though I didn't want to disappoint Jayasimha by telling him so: cow shelters in which a cow will spend her entire life tied on a short rope to a stake in the ground in the darkness of a shed, periodically milked. Of all the things I have seen, the one thing I wish I could unsee was that. Saved from slaughter, yes, but for what? For life itself. For profit. To perform one's humanity. Here, at least, the cows could move, but they were jammed together and sickly, gray from the urban pollution. We went to the top story, where there was one rather pristine-looking, snow-white calf. There was a bloody wound on her shoulder, though, the size and depth of a softball, and it was full of wriggling yellow maggots, the infection clearly spreading. Jayasimha found someone from management and showed him the wound. The man shrugged: "Maggots are also life." It was the closest I had ever seen Jayasimha to being angry. But it would turn out that he shares something with this man: an emotive response to vitality that shades intriguingly into, and out of, a critique of speciesism.

A few weeks into my time in Hyderabad, Jayasimha and I went to Nagaland, one of the seven states in northeastern India. The region is conflict ridden and impoverished, with active Maoist and separatist movements. People here often identify less culturally with the Indian mainland than with China and Tibet. Even Bollywood has little influence here. The population is largely tribal and Christian. A *Times of India* reporter had been wanting for months to take a trip to Nagaland with Jayasimha to investigate the trade in dog meat. It would be a sensational story; the Othering of northeasterners by mainland Indians is often on the basis of their supposed affinity for eating dog and rat. (When, for example, Delhi University increased its seats for northeastern students, rumors began circulating about the drastic decline in the number of dogs on campus.) Jayasimha was only interested insofar as it was an excuse for us to go to Nagaland. His formula made this plain: his time would be better spent getting Hyderabadis to eat fewer eggs and cutting into the ninety-five million layer hens produced in Indian hatcheries every year, or even getting farmers to go cage-free, than to chase after Nagas who eat a dog on special occasions. Sentiment is no good in Jayasimha's world, not in a time and place of accelerated consumption.

The journalist, ultimately, couldn't come, so it was just the two of us. We woke up at 4:30 a.m. to make it to the market as the animals came in. It was cold and gray and drizzling, with a smell of smoke in the air. As we approached the first still-shuttered shops, a black Jeep came rumbling down the road, stopping right next to us. In the back were giant pigs, more yellowish than pink, cut right down the middle. They were heaved onto the counter by two men. The animal halves jiggled as they crashed down, gargantuan, heavy, and fleshy. The back legs were splayed; the front legs were together in front of the chest, held as if in prayer but actually just from having been tied like that. The ropes were gone now that the animal was long dead. The eyes of this one were squeezed so tightly shut that there were barely slits there. Jayasimha said softly to me as we walked on, past the buckets full of eel and goats being stripped, that there were no other wound marks on any of the pigs. They had just been sawed to death. More Jeeps came rumbling down, now with cows, also all in half, their hooves and lower legs bouncing over the back of the vehicle, spread, hips wide and feminine. One man was working on a cow head, the top of the head on the stump. The cow's gray tongue was sticking out of its mouth, its eyes open, as the man cleaved through it, gradually prying it open with his hands.

The dogs, we found out from the mutton man, were killed in the back, below ground. We went in where he pointed, ducking under hanging chains, and the smell of smoke became stronger. There were no people there, no animals that we could see, just bloody crates covered with cardboard and plastic, all seemingly empty. There were small doors along the left side wall, all latched. The entire place was cobwebbed and lit by a naked bulb. When my eyes adjusted I saw on one of the wooden stumps to my left an animal—a small one, on its back, its legs in rigor mortis, roasted black and brown with bits of pink and golden yellow. Its mouth was open and you could see tiny teeth. This had been a dog.

Two women, nicely dressed (I had seen them alight from a taxi earlier and thought to myself, what nice perfume they were wearing), and a man emerged at the back of the room. You kill the dogs here, we asked? Yeah, one of the women said, we're doing them now, come down. The stairs were muddy and uneven, and there was little to hold on to, so we made our way carefully. What can I say about what I saw there? It was kind of like a village under a highway overpass. Though covered, it looked out over a swamp of moldy water and garbage, the swamp at least two stories down from where we stood. On the other side of the swamp, about a hundred yards away, was a large silver billboard. I don't remember what it said, just that it seemed incongruous. There were two women with blowtorches, sitting on their haunches, both of them torching dead dogs with their flame. They worked intently and sometimes said things that made the other laugh.

There was one living dog here: a furry-eared mountain dog with a dark nose and innocent eyes looking at us. He was mostly inside of a sack but his head was sticking out and he was sitting upright. A couple of times he breathed very deeply, like a sigh. There were piles and piles of sacks just behind him, but they appeared to be empty. Two dogs, killed before we arrived, were dropped in. Someone began torching one right in front of the living dog, and for the first time I saw alarm in his face. He looked up at me. I looked back and then looked away. The smell of burning hair became so intense that Jayasimha feared he would wretch and asked if we could go up for some air.

The air was better up here, back in the market, where things had gotten much busier. We stood near a chicken stall. A skinny adolescent boy was in charge of this one, and he was struggling to keep up with the demand. The more experienced butchers, as we had seen earlier that morning, take the bird by the base of the wings with the left hand, raise their right fist in the air, and bring it crashing down onto the chicken's back with a deep thud. This breaks a rib which pierces the heart and kills the bird almost instantly. This skinny boy also grabbed a bird with his left hand. He raised his right fist and then just started punching the bird, its head, its body. He had no clue what he was doing. I heard Jayasimha gasp, and I turned around with surprise. What could he have seen, this man of many slaughterhouses, that made him gasp like that? It was the chicken being punched, by a butcher boy who hadn't a clue.

While all this was happening, a cage arrived with several pigeons in it and a few rats. A man opened the cage from the top and took a rat out, asking if we wanted one. We shook our heads no. He tied one back foot of the rat with a long string and put it down on the ground and watched with great interest and some excitement as it struggled to run away, struggled to burrow itself into a hole in the ground. I waited, horrified: was he going to step on it?[15] But he was just watching, and so were a few other men, and they laughed as they watched the rat struggle. They did this with another rat, too, and then took them both away.

A woman rushed past us and said with a laugh, *Maar denge!* (we're going to kill that dog!). Jayasimha rushed down, and I went after him. I was too late to see her actually grab the dog and drag it, in its gunny sack, to the edge of the world. But I arrived in time to see all of this: the dog being placed so that it faced the market's silver billboard and the large swamp of moldy water and garbage that lay between. The strangest thing about it is how it looked in that sack, like it was in a blanket, and how noble it looked (to me) staring off into the distance, with its furry head and ears. The woman picked up a club, swung it up to her right, and brought it down onto the dog's quiet head. I wondered what it was thinking just then, what was the last thing it saw. She tossed the body over to the side where I could no longer see it. But from the fact that she stood watching it was obvious that he still had life in his body. When she was certain that he no longer did, she pulled the body out from the sack and tossed it toward the blowtorcher.

We arrived at the airport in Dimapur a few hours before our flight home. I typed up notes, and Jayasimha watched *The Big Bang Theory* on his laptop. I finally asked him how he was feeling. He nodded slowly, not ready to give anything away. I said I was upset. I thought I would never forget the back of that dog's head as it looked out into the open across the swamp, toward the silver billboard, smoke from burning flesh rising up behind him. What was the last thing he saw? What was he thinking? Jayasimha acknowledged that he was bothered, too, but more than anything by the rat. The rat, I said. That's interesting. He nodded again. "None of the other animals we saw were struggling. Not the chickens, really, not the dog. But the *rat*. The rat was desperate to *live*."

A rat is a dog is a chicken? Yes and no. His response was not, as it was for me, and maybe would have been for Abodh, about sentiment, about favoring with love the promising animal that reflects back to me my own humanity. Nor was his response like the gaushala manager's, though on the face of it, it is life above all that they both value.[16] "Maggots are also life," the gaushala manager said, implicitly adding, "just like this snow-white calf." But this is what I hoped *not* to make of Arpan's statement, the assertion of a radical equivalency: a maggot is *the same as* a calf, and therefore we must respect each, always, precisely, and consistently. There is no ethics here because there is no concept of, no space for, differentiation, immanent or otherwise. Why, then, is what Jayasimha says different? Well, for him a "rat" is not the *same* as a "dog." Those categories themselves mean nothing here. What matters is vitality. The vital rat that draws him in today might be a vital dog tomorrow. And yet, none of this really matters because he was not asked to extinguish the dog so that the rat could live. But had he been asked? Well, then his utilitarian formula would kick in: how much bang for my buck—not how *much life*, but how *many lives*? And we are back not to speciesism but to radical equivalency. But actually what we are brought back to is the maggot. The maggot was our limit case: proof that we are doomed to love (discriminate) and therefore to violence; proof that our ethics are always imperfect, inconsistent. But so what?

Erika is a woman I know in Udaipur, Rajasthan. She lives there with her husband, Jim, and their adult daughter, Claire. They're from Seattle. They have given their lives to animals. People refer to Erika, in particular, as a god, a tireless animal whisperer. (I should acknowledge, before I go further, the racial and postcolonial politics here: it is possible to read this as a white woman saving animals from brown people. And as I discuss elsewhere, animal activism in India is indeed inseparable from a longer imperial history of liberalism, or white people saving brown women from brown men.[17] I offer, however, two caveats. First, as Leela Gandhi has shown, animal activism in India has also been part of a radical practice of anticolonialism.[18] Second, something being true—in this case, the inseparability of contemporary animal rights activism in India with an imperial affective legacy—must not render it the only truth worth acknowledging: something is not everything, nor is it nothing.) They run a shelter and just last year decided to go all in, moving even their home to the shelter, right in the middle of the three-legged dogs and the paralyzed pigs and the nighttime car accident cow emergencies. There will be nothing left between them and heartbreak, them and their labor. We all spent many hours together talking. Erika told me about how she got into this work, through a woman named Christine Townsend who ran a legendary shelter in Jaipur, the one Timmie Kumar later ran. Erika was overwhelmed: Where to start? Where to end? The woman's response, Erika said, was the most important piece of advice she has ever received: "Just don't do nothing." Interestingly, we had all spent the previous night talking about just this. Claire spoke of never feeling that you've done enough, for every moment carrying a dog around in her arms, there was so much else she was choosing against: breaking into a lab, doing undercover work at a slaughterhouse. But somewhere she knew this: to try to do everything, to try to do anything more than this, would be to be consumed by one's own fire, to knowingly kill the place that the love comes from.

Animal activists talk about this descent into obligation. There is an actress in Hyderabad whom everyone simply calls Amala. She has been working for animals for the last twenty-odd years. She told me, in narrating her story, though only when I pressed her by way of asking about her meditation practice, about the "dark hour of the soul that every activist goes through," of how working with animals is "a never-ending, bottomless ocean."[19] This was just a month after I had met Timmie, and Amala reminded me of her words, of her persistent fear that she would "drown from knowing too much." "I have to stop now," Timmie had said. "I didn't want to do nothing. But somehow nothing became everything, and I started to drown."

Something

There were two shrugs in this essay. The first shrug was Dipesh's: his shrug, after I screamed, thinking the dog with armadillo skin would be hit by a car. His shrug, after extracting maggots from her ass, was to say, "She's old." The second shrug was at the gaushala in Hyderabad: the snow-white calf on the top level of the bovine parking garage with a maggoty wound the size of a softball. The manager's shrug was to say, "Maggots are also life." This shrug says, everything lives. Dipesh's shrug says, everything dies. Two shrugs, two philosophies. Interestingly, the shrug that says everything dies is the ground for action. The shrug that says everything lives is the ground for something else. And so this is what I want to say, about the maggot and what it signifies when we say to Dipesh, "But what about the maggots?" We say, like the gaushala manager, "Maggots are also life; everything lives," and like Claire's fire and like Amala's ocean and like Timmie's yawning abyss between nothing and everything (these are her only options), we choose the everything that will swallow us whole, a void where everything is the same and so nothing can be extinguished—not maggots, not cows, not horror, not love. Is "everything" the ethics of our moment? Must we lock in our broom closet cows and dogs—everything accumulated for an uncertain future? Nothing can be extinguished; nothing can be deleted.

But that's not what most of us mean when we ask, what about the maggots? We ask, what is the point of healing that, of not eating this, when there is everywhere extinction? What is the logic here? And I, an animal, can only shrug.

Notes

1. Sloterdijk, *Critique of Cynical Reason*, 379.

2. Povinelli, "Will to Be Otherwise."

3. See Povinelli, *Economies of Abandonment*. Elizabeth Povinelli locates immanent obligation in the tense of the "durative present." Lauren Berlant, in a special lecture delivered at the 2012 American Anthropological Association meeting, put forward the concept of "elliptical life," which is also a dwelling in the durative present that "shrugs" at futural or communal promises. See Berlant, "Elliptical Life"; and Byler, "Walking Around."

4. The premise of this phrase is familiar to many animal rights activists. Ingrid Newkirk, founder of People for the Ethical Treatment of Animals, famously said in 1989 that a "rat is a pig is a dog is a boy." She explained that for animal liberationists, all mammals, or even anything with a nervous system, is of equal value.

5. Dave, "Love and Other Injustices."

6. Also at issue here—and signaled by Arpan's practice of meditation (see also Amala, later)—is the deliberate cultivation of detachment as a means to avoid both a descent into obligation and specific partialities. See Matei Candea's essay on detachment as a form of engagement among animal activists, "Engagement and Detachment."

7. Major arguments in favor of animal rights tend to be, for obvious reasons (they are, after all, "arguments"), rationalist. Peter Singer's utilitarianism in *Animal Liberation*, Tom Regan's Kantian imperative toward any "subject-of-a-life" in *The Case for Animal Rights*, Will Kymlicka and Sue Donaldson's political theory of disparate right and obligation in "Animals and the Frontiers of Citizenship," Marjorie Spiegel's *Dreaded Comparison* of animal exploitation with slavery or the Holocaust, and even J. M. Coetzee's collection *The Lives of Animals* and Jacques Derrida's *The Animal That Therefore I Am* are examples of how our treatment of animals becomes premised on our accepting a truth and then acting on it as logically and consistently as we can. Even what we would consider more "affective" arguments for ethical encounters with Others, such as feminist care theory (e.g., Donovan, "Feminism and the Treatment of Animals"), Emmanuel Levinas's theory of the face that compels obligation (the sort of face an animal does not have) in "Paradox of Morality," or Stanley Cavell's "Companionable Thinking"—a focus on being in common with others—that might include such different thinkers as Donna Haraway (*When Species Meet*) and Veena Das ("Violence and Nonviolence") are based on acting or not acting for a reason. I acknowledge and even usually appreciate that we act for reasons and with reason, but I also want to ask, with Cora Diamond ("Difficulty of Reality"), concerning animal ethics, how much of our reasoned debates are about limiting our exposure to the world rather than opening ourselves up to previously unimagined, immanent ethical responsibility.

8. Pandey, "Rallying round the Cow"; Lodrick, *Sacred Cows*; Jha, *Myth of the Holy Cow*; Doniger, *On Hinduism*; Chigateri, "'Glory to the Cow'"; Das, "Violence and Nonviolence."

9. See Massumi, *What Animals Teach Us about Politics*.

10. Dave, "Love and Other Injustices."

11. Fassin, *Humanitarian Reason*.

12. See Ticktin, "Non-human Suffering"; and Derrida, *The Animal That Therefore I Am*.

13. It is tempting to Indianize this. For instance, I could say that the conflation of animal rights activism with humanitarian reason assumes a Western model of action, with the associated (if contradictory) "Western" affects: liberal sentimentality, salvation, reason. And then I could say: but here we have Dipesh, an animal activist who operates from within a different regime, one we might call broadly Indic, encompassing Buddhist and Hindu thought with their varying emphases on detachment from outcome (usually associated with Buddhism, though the *Bhagavad Gita* makes a similar demand). The problem with that line of argument is that it does nothing to unsettle the tyranny of consistency. It would be a product of *my* closet tyrant (or anthropology's not-so-closet one) insisting that, however inconsistent his actions might appear to some, they are perfectly consistent within his own religio-spiritual-cultural context. My aim, however, is not to make Dipesh consistent; that is, my aim is not to explain him away (see Strathern, "Out of Context"). Like Timmie, Abodh, Arpan, and Chauhan (and like Jayasimha and Amala, whom I introduce later), certainly Dipesh's life is shaped by Indic thought. But another thing they all share, as actors who act otherwise, is subjection to the tyranny of consistency. Some, like Dipesh, shrug at it, while others are paralyzed or drown in it. Either way, it is the insistence on consistency that this article rejects, by allowing for an ethics that is (even if inconsistently) immanent—an ethics no less Indic after all than Western (no less Buddhist, say, than Spinozan). I elaborate on the relationship between contradiction and context in Dave, "On Contradiction."

14. Povinelli, "'Enduring in the Verge.'"

15. Clearly I have been affected by Hugh Raffles. See Raffles, *Insectopedia*.

16. The words and deeds of this particular Jain in this encounter represent something important about Jain animal politics but of course do not exhaust the complexity of Jain thought about what constitutes life. I am persuaded by James Laidlaw, who in fact stresses that Jain ethics are not rationalist or axiomatic. Yes, Jains would agree that both a maggot and a calf have a soul and that both have the capacity to suffer. But believing this, and even practicing this by not killing the maggot, is not ethically sufficient; ethical self-formation for Jains depends on imaginatively (not logically) cultivating an experience of the world that is full of invisible life and suffering and acting based on that visceral imaginative experience. I would just say that this gaushala manager, by not killing the maggots, is acting consistently with Jain practice but not necessarily with Jain moral thought. Laidlaw, "Ethical Traditions in Question."

17. Dave, "Witness"; Spivak, "Can the Subaltern Speak?"

18. Gandhi, *Affective Communities*.

19. Fearing she had sounded too negative, Amala e-mailed me weeks later to remind me that all is not dark in this world and that she owes much to those who worked before her and who continue to do good work for animals.

References

Berlant, Lauren. 2012. "Elliptical Life." Paper presented at the annual meeting of the American Anthropological Association, San Francisco, 17 November.

Byler, Darren. 2012. "Walking Around in Lauren Berlant's 'Elliptical Life.'" *Cultural Anthropology* (blog), 10 December. www.culanth.org/fieldsights/32-walking-around-in-lauren-berlant-s-elliptical-life.

Candea, Matei. 2010. "'I Fell in Love with Carlos the Meerkat': Engagement and Detachment in Human–Animal Relations." *American Ethnologist* 37, no. 2: 241–58.

Cavell, Stanley. 2008. "Companionable Thinking." In *Philosophy and Animal Life*, edited by Stanley Cavell, Cora Diamond, John McDowell, Ian Hacking, and Cary Wolfe, 91–126. New York: Columbia University Press.

Chigateri, Shraddha. 2008. "'Glory to the Cow': Cultural Difference and Social Justice in the Food Hierarchy in India." *South Asia: Journal of South Asian Studies* 31, no. 1: 10–35.

Coetzee, J. M., ed. 1999. *The Lives of Animals*. Princeton, NJ: Princeton University Press.

Das, Veena. 2013. "Violence and Nonviolence at the Heart of Hindu Ethics." In *The Oxford Handbook of Religion and Violence*, edited by Margo Kitts, Mark Juergensmeyer, and Michael Jerryson. New York: Oxford University Press. www.oxfordhandbooks.com/view/10.1093/oxfordhb/9780199759996.001.0001/oxfordhb-9780199759996-e-1

Dave, Naisargi N. 2014. "Witness: Humans, Animals, and the Politics of Becoming." *Cultural Anthropology* 29, no. 3: 433–56.

Dave, Naisargi N. 2016. "Love and Other Injustices: On Indifference to Difference." Franklin Humanities Institute Papers, Duke University. humanitiesfutures.org/papers/845/ (accessed 6 July 2016).

Dave, Naisargi N. 2016. "On Contradiction: Humans, Animals, and 'The Way Things Are.'" Paper delivered at the Anthropology Colloquium, Princeton University, 3 March.

Derrida, Jacques. 2008. *The Animal That Therefore I Am*. New York: Fordham University Press.

Diamond, Cora. 2008. "The Difficulty of Reality and the Difficulty of Philosophy." In *Philosophy and Animal Life*, edited by Stanley Cavell, Cora Diamond, John McDowell, Ian Hacking, and Cary Wolfe, 43–90. New York: Columbia University Press.

Doniger, Wendy. 2014. *On Hinduism*. New York: Oxford University Press.

Donovan, Josephine. 2006. "Feminism and the Treatment of Animals: From Care to Dialogue." *Signs: Journal of Women in Culture and Society* 31, no. 2: 305–29.

Fassin, Didier. 2012. *Humanitarian Reason: A Moral History of the Present*. Berkeley: University of California Press.

Gandhi, Leela. 2006. *Affective Communities: Anticolonial Thought, Fin-de-Siècle Radicalism, and the Politics of Friendship*. Durham, NC: Duke University Press.

Haraway, Donna. 2008. *When Species Meet*. Minneapolis: University of Minnesota Press.

Jha, D. N. 2002. *The Myth of the Holy Cow*. London: Verso.

Kymlicka, Will, and Sue Donaldson. 2014. "Animals and the Frontiers of Citizenship." *Oxford Journal of Legal Studies* 34, no. 2: 201–19.

Laidlaw, James. 2010. "Ethical Traditions in Question: Diaspora Jainism and the Environmental and Animal Liberation Movements." In *Ethical Life in South Asia*, edited by Anand Pandian and Daud Ali, 61–82. Bloomington: Indiana University Press.

Levinas, Emmanuel. 2004. "The Paradox of Morality." In *Animal Philosophy: Essential Readings in Continental Thought*, edited by Matthew Calarco. New York: Continuum Press.

Lodrick, Deryck O. 1981. *Sacred Cows, Sacred Places: Origins and Survivals of Animal Homes in India*. Berkeley: University of California Press.

Massumi, Brian. 2014. *What Animals Teach Us about Politics*. Durham, NC: Duke University Press.

Pandey, Gyan. 1983. "Rallying round the Cow: Sectarian Strife in the Bhojpuri Region, c. 1888–1917." In *Subaltern Studies*, vol. 2, edited by F. Robinson and J. McLane, 60–129. Oxford: Oxford University Press.

Povinelli, Elizabeth. 2011. *Economies of Abandonment: Social Belonging and Endurance in Late Liberalism*. Durham, NC: Duke University Press.

Povinelli, Elizabeth. 2012. "'Enduring in the Verge': Discussant Commentary." Paper presented at the annual meeting of the American Anthropological Association, San Francisco, 17 November.

Povinelli, Elizabeth. 2012. "The Will to Be Otherwise/the Effort of Endurance." *South Atlantic Quarterly* 111, no. 3: 453–75.

Raffles, Hugh. 2010. *Insectopedia*. New York: Pantheon Books.

Regan, Tom. 2004. *The Case for Animal Rights*. Berkeley: University of California Press.

Singer, Peter. 1975. *Animal Liberation: A New Ethics for the Treatment of Our Animals*. New York: New York Review.

Sloterdijk, Peter. 1988. *Critique of Cynical Reason*. Minneapolis: University of Minnesota Press.

Spiegel, Marjorie. 1997. *The Dreaded Comparison: Human and Animal Slavery*. New York: Mirror Books.

Spivak, Gayatri Chakravorty. 1988. "Can the Subaltern Speak?" In *Marxism and the Interpretation of Culture*, edited by Cary Nelson and Lawrence Grossberg, 271–313. Urbana: University of Illinois Press.

Strathern, Marilyn. 1987. "Out of Context: The Persuasive Fictions of Anthropology." *Current Anthropology* 28, no. 3: 251–81.

Ticktin, Miriam. 2015. "Non-human Suffering: A Humanitarian Project." In *The Clinic and the Courtroom*, edited by Tobias Kelly, Ian Harper, and Akshay Khanna, 49–71. Cambridge: Cambridge University Press.

Sounding Death, Saying Something

Lisa Stevenson

In his famous "fort–da" scene, Sigmund Freud,[1] that brilliant ethnographer of the everyday, describes a child (his grandson) with a spool tied to a piece of string who repeatedly throws the spool out of his crib and then joyfully reels it back in. Throwing and retrieving the spool is the child's response to the temporary departure of his mother; Freud says that in this way the child reexperiences and gains a sense of mastery over his mother's absence. Yet the psychoanalyst D. W. Winnicott tells us that at a certain point in child development the absence of the mother *is* death for the child: "This is what dead means."[2]

In this essay I am interested in what it might mean to send one's voice across or into such absences that *are* death. In particular, I want to think about a series of tape-recorded messages made in 1961 of Inuit in Arctic Canada sending messages to their relatives in tuberculosis sanatoria in southern Canada some two thousand miles away.

During the tuberculosis epidemic of the 1950s and 1960s, Inuit diagnosed with tuberculosis (most of whom were living in small communities around the Hudson Bay posts or military posts scattered around the Arctic) were immediately evacuated from the North by boat, plane, and/or train. The dislocation the evacuations caused was severe. Families who had never been apart were separated, sometimes for years at a time. Children were separated from parents, and husbands from wives, with little means of communication. It was impossible to know for sure if your relative in a southern sanatorium was alive or dead.

By the mid-1950s the Department of Northern Affairs began a program to tape-record messages between Inuit in hospital and their relatives. The audio recordings I am concerned with in this essay were made by a nurse who went north with the medical team on the ship the *C. D. Howe* in 1961 and recorded family members speaking to their relatives in

Social Text 130 · Vol. 35, No. 1 · March 2017
DOI 10.1215/01642472-3727996 © 2017 Duke University Press

the Mountain Sanatorium in Hamilton, Ontario. Many of the Inuit on the tape had a hard time finding words to speak into the recorder. For example, a daughter says to her mother, "I don't know what to say, Mom, so I'm just going to say hello and bye, Mom." Nonetheless (and this seems crucial to me), the Inuit lent their voices to the project: they spoke into the recorder.

In this essay, by juxtaposing these "soundings" (of Inuit speaking onto the tape) with some dreams Inuit youth have of their dead friends and linking these to some Inuit songs and poetry collected by explorers of the early twentieth century, I want to think about the possibility of "sending" our voices to the absent/dead and the way they, the dead, send their voices to us.

"To Make Them Well"

The tuberculosis epidemic that spread through Inuit communities of the Canadian Arctic in the 1950s and 1960s was fierce. So was the campaign "to make them well."[3] By 1956 one out of every seven Inuit in Canada was in a southern tuberculosis sanatorium. By the early 1960s almost 50 percent of the population had spent time in a southern sanatorium. Inuit were taken from a life that revolved around hunting and trapping—families lived either in skin tents, *iglus*, and *qarmaqs* (sod houses) on the land or in small communities located around the Hudson Bay Company outposts or military encampments—and relocated to hospitals in southern Canada. The transition from a life in the Arctic to the cement, glass, and medical machinery of a hospital was swift and disorienting. One week they were hunting whale and walrus, and then after an arduous and unfamiliar trip by a ship or plane, and then train or bus, they were sipping apple juice from a straw in a hospital cot. The trip itself was grueling. As the anthropologist Robert Williamson recalled later, "It was terrible because it was the ship which carried the Inuit away from their homes to the sanatoria in the south. And they were herded together . . . in three-tiered bunks, mass-fed, mass-accommodated. In the stormy seas they were sick, they were terrified, they were demoralized. They were frightened."[4] The decision to remove Inuit from their homes was made by medical personnel (including an X-ray technician and his assistant) who traveled north on the yearly rounds of the *C. D. Howe*, the Royal Canadian Mounted Police patrol boat. The *C. D. Howe* made calls in all the Inuit settlements of the region. At each stop Inuit were brought on board and X-rayed. Once on the ship, the X-ray films were developed immediately and the transparencies mined for irregularities. In the early years, when a dark shadow appeared in the pulmonary region the patient was instructed to stay aboard. Everyone else was ordered off. Children were separated from mothers, and husbands from wives, with very little explanation of what was going on. An interpreter described the scene: "But they'd run away—they try to hide and not be there. It was always sad. It was disgusting, the whole thing was disgusting. We were just breaking into their lives. . . . We didn't leave them any choice."[5]

By 1956 the sanatorium in Hamilton, Ontario, known as "Mountain San" housed 332 Inuit, the largest community of Inuit anywhere in Canada. For those Inuit sent to southern Canada, their longing to return home was often overwhelming. Many Inuit wrote letters (in Inuktitut) to government officials they had met in the North begging them to let them return: "I am the only one who can take care of my family right now. Here I am just in bed. . . . I want to go home now, even though I am not totally cured. I don't hardly sleep anymore at nights. I am finding it a long time to get home."[6] Some Inuit never made it back and were given a pauper's burial in unmarked graves in nearby cemeteries. In 1952 one man, David Mikeyook, was so distressed at being told he could not return to his family that he simply walked out of Mountain San wearing his pajamas and armed with a pocketknife. His body was found two months later beside a nearby ravine.[7]

In the personal archives of a ninety-four-year-old anthropologist, Toshio Yatsushiro, who worked with the Inuit in the 1950s,[8] I found such a letter written by an Inuit man named Quvianaqtuq.[9] The letter, dated October 1958, was written in Inuktitut syllabics. It pleaded with the anthropologist (understood by Quvianaqtuq to be an agent of the Canadian state) to understand that Inuit were not like the Qallunaat (white people). The Inuit, unlike the Qallunaat, could not bear to be away from their families for long periods of time. Quvianaqtuq stressed that the nurses and doctors were good people, working tirelessly to make Inuit live longer, but he admitted that he could not understand why otherwise good people would send Inuit away to hospitals in the South. He is forced to conclude that it must be out of the doctors' control: "I know you all have bosses and you are supposed to follow certain rules," he writes. "Do so, for the good of the people and explain to us what they mean. We will try to cooperate and some of us will write it down so we won't forget."

How to make sense of the medical bureaucracy, which from the outset privileged living longer over living in community, was not a straightforward task. Bryan Pearson, then a member of the Northwest Territories governing council (the precursor to the Legislative Assembly), told a Canadian Broadcast Corporation reporter a related story about a three-month-old baby who was taken from her family and sent south for tuberculosis treatment. Twelve years later, out of the blue, the child appeared at their doorstep accompanied by a social worker. "Here is your daughter, we brought her back for you," announces the social worker.

"We don't have a daughter. We never had one," the couple replies.

"Well, yes you did, but that was a long time ago."

To which the family replies, "Yes, but she died. The white man took her away and she died. We've never heard of her since."[10]

The Canadian Broadcast Corporation reporter was somewhat skeptical about the story. But what did he doubt? Was it the fact that a three-month-old baby could be separated from its family for twelve years without a word of news, or was it that her family would no longer recognize her? Pearson, a longtime resident of the North and a great advocate of the Inuit, maintained that he had heard several such stories and that this story was true. What the story seems to ask us to consider is the relationship between life and community.

Leah Idlout, an Inuit woman who had spent years in the South recovering from tuberculosis, later reworked a Dr. Seuss story, *Horton Hatches the Egg*, into a story for Inuit children.[11] In Idlout's version of the story, a polar bear and a tern become friends. The polar bear tends to the tern's egg while the tern goes off hunting for seals. But the tern never returns, having, little by little, been drawn south for the winter. The bear is left to hatch the tern's egg himself. The creature that finally emerges from the egg is part bear and part bird. That exotic bear-bird is soon kidnapped and taken to a circus in the Deep South, and the story ends there with the bear-bird singing:

> Again, again, it's going to snow.
> How do we know it's going to snow?
> Because it's always snowed before.[12]

But of course it *won't* snow. For me, this story traces the line of this tragedy: to find oneself in a world so altered that something that has always happened will never happen again. But that knowledge is so devastating that it can't be spoken aloud. "Again, again, it's going to snow," sings the bear-bird from its well-appointed cage in the circus.

When Idlout boarded the *C. D. Howe* in Pond Inlet in 1951 to begin her journey to the Mountain Sanatorium in Hamilton, Ontario, she had had less than three hours to prepare herself. She was eleven years old, and her whole life up until that point had been lived in her family's traditional hunting camps: "All I had ever seen of [the white man's land] were the colored pictures in *Life* magazine, full of dead bodies lying on the ground, wounded men, scenes of war with the Japanese, the families of the Queen and King George VI, the Russians, and so on."[13] She feared that she herself would die in the hospital. As the ship moved away from the harbor, "there were so many white people lined up on the upper deck, watching as the *C. D. Howe* moved away from the settlement. I tried hard to hold back my tears, at the same time straining to keep sight of my father's boat until I could hardly tell which one was my mom or dad."[14]

Idlout's story of the bear-bird, ending with it being kidnapped by a circus, partakes of a tradition of Inuit storytelling in which redemption of any kind, and happy endings specifically, are not required. For example, one story collected by an early ethnographer provides an image of murderous love: a father hugs his baby so hard he tears her head off. Another tells of a mother who kills and flays her own daughter. The mother then dons her daughter's skin to trick the girl's husband into drawing close so that she can kill him too. But the husband escapes and manages somehow to return to his parents' camp. They, however, are so overjoyed to see him that they drop dead.[15] Or, in the celebrated Inuit story of Sedna, the spirit of the sea, the young Sedna is tricked into marrying a fulmar who treats her cruelly. She finally escapes with her father in a kayak after her father manages to kill the fulmar. But the fulmar's bird-friends take revenge by causing a massive storm to overtake the kayak. To survive, the father throws his daughter into the sea. As she clings to the side of the boat asking for help, her father cuts off her fingers at the first joints. When she manages to grab hold again, he cuts them off at the next joint. In these stories protagonists often continue to suffer, even at the tale's end. Suffering doesn't bring peace or happiness or justice, and death doesn't redeem.[16]

When Idlout was discharged from the sanatorium, she, like many Inuit patients, did not return immediately to her family. Instead she was taken in by a white, and very kind, foster family who tried to permanently adopt her. Idlout's father held firm in the face of kindness—he insisted that his daughter be returned home. Idlout has since been haunted by the sense that she was neither fully Inuit nor fully white.

The kinds of stories the medical professionals told about the evacuations had only happy endings and happy, contented Inuit patients. In fact, the Inuit experience of the tuberculosis evacuations was often obscured by the optimism, eloquence, and kindness of the medical reports. For example, a doctor interviewed on a 1959 radio broadcast confidently reported that "it has not been too difficult, particularly of latter years, to convince these people that it is for their own good, for the protection of the rest of their family, that they should take advantage of the white man's offer to make them well again."[17] The superintendent of the Mountain Sanatorium, Dr. Hugo Ewart (who was instrumental in facilitating the production of tape-recorded messages by Inuit), told a Canadian Broadcast Corporation reporter that, while the people responsible for the evacuations did sometimes wonder whether they were doing the right thing, there was no "actual debate" about whether bringing Inuit from the far North to southern hospitals for treatment was the best solution to the problem. There was no debate, because, according to Ewart, "there was no alternative. They did not have the hospitals in the North. The treatment was long and drawn out, and we had the beds, and we had the capabilities, and were willing to do it. Therefore we brought them down." Ewart went on to tell the story of an old Inuit man with drug-resistant tuberculosis who was kept in hospital twenty-seven years before he died: "The old man was perfectly happy when he was told that this was in his lungs, and if he went back, he would cough these little worms at the children around, and they would get them, and he never complained again."[18]

A Canadian Broadcast Corporation television news program from 1956 shows smiling Inuit women at the Mountain Sanatorium industriously sewing parkas, belts, and boots and men making soapstone carvings. Inuit children are seen in the hospital schoolroom learning to read and write. The voice-over says in a kind voice, "The younger patients are given regular schooling in English and other basic subjects. Their summertime teacher says they're the most cooperative and willing students she's ever had."[19]

The Tapes

In 2006 I visited the archives of Hamilton Health Sciences and Faculty of Health Science at McMaster University. I wanted to hear the tape of messages from Inuit families for myself, and I wanted to get a sense of the large collection of photographs of Inuit in hospital stored in that archive. Once I arrived, I arranged with the archivist to send the audiotape to the national archives in Ottawa to be digitized.

The tape in the McMaster archives contains five messages from family members in the communities of Lake Harbour, Arctic Bay, Pond Inlet, and Clyde River to patients in the Hamilton Sanatorium in Ontario, approximately two thousand miles away. Each message, recorded in Inuktitut, is introduced by the voice of a nurse, speaking in English. Her voice, calm and contained, has a way of putting things in order. Each message is numbered; each speaker is identified by his or her Inuktitut name along with a government-issued disc number. The recipient of the message is also named, and a disc number also given.

Still, many of the Inuit being recorded had a hard time finding words to speak into the recorder. A mother says to her son: "S., your mom speaking. I'm just going to say 'Bye' to you right now." And then her voice breaks off. "What was it?" She says softly, as if searching for a scattered thought. Then briskly she starts again, as if there had been no problem. "I don't know what to say. Just listen and do as you're told. That's all." She ends abruptly, the same way you would end a call on a CB radio. "Taima!" Over and out.

A father says to his daughter, "This is your father speaking E5-346.

Although I don't have much to say. Though I'm not with you and can't see you physically I would like to say to you that although I don't know how you are I try not to worry about you too much."

A father ends his brief message to his son saying, "I'm not quite sure what to say for now so I'll say bye for now."

A very small child says in a frightened voice: "Goodbye." And then, with a little coaching, he says, "Big brother, goodbye."[20]

In the 1950s and 1960s, getting messages to and from Inuit in hospital was difficult. There were no telephones in Inuit homes, and the mail came only sporadically. One message, recorded by a patient in 1956 in the Hamilton Sanatorium in Ontario,[21] for her mother living in Pangnirtung (in what is now Nunavut Territory), addressed the possibility that the messages might never make it to their recipients: "Maybe you will hear this or maybe you won't," said the young girl into the recorder. "Anyway, do not worry about me. I do not fret at this end."

Inuit who died in hospital were usually buried in unmarked graves in the nearby cemetery. Although hospital staff tried to inform the families of their deaths, there was often much confusion about the identity of the Inuit in hospital, especially the children. Hospital administrators, like some Northern Service Officers, could not speak Inuktitut and had no clear sense of arctic geography.

There were also those stories, like the one I recounted above concerning Leah Idlout, of children being removed from hospital and not being sent back to their parents, being placed instead in foster homes without the permission or even the knowledge of their parents. Those stories seem to have no end. One man I interviewed in Arctic Bay returned home to find out his *atiq* or name-soul had been given away—his parents believed he was dead, and his name had been given to another child. Martha Michaels of Iqaluit has described waiting for news of her sister who went away to be treated for tuberculosis and was never heard from again: "I used to always expect Napatsie to come back. When we first got telephones I thought about receiving a call from someone that she is still alive. You really don't want to believe she's dead when you've never seen the grave."[22]

For the Inuit speaking into the recorder, the status of the family member in hospital, as dead or alive, would have been fundamentally uncertain: still alive *probably*, dying *possibly*, dead without the message having arrived—*not impossible*. The everyday relationship between absence and death is illuminated here. Do we ever really know whether the people we love will come back to us dead or alive?

In listening to the tapes, I was struck by the repetition of the phrase "I don't know what to say." The impossibility of saying something, of having some*thing* to say into that absence-that-is-death, becomes manifest. This is not to minimize the fact that there was certainly a sense of embarrassment or shyness that came over someone in speaking into a large and unfamiliar machine in the presence of a nurse who spoke formally and authoritatively into the recorder. But notwithstanding that, what is there to say, exactly, to someone who is absent/dead, who may or may not return, who is a child, a mother, a lover?

It seems to me as if speakers ran up against, on the one hand, the impossibility of saying *something* and, on the other hand, the importance of *saying* something—the importance of speaking itself. They lend their voices to the project, not knowing whether their words will reach the person they address, but also not knowing *what* to say.

For Freud, in the story of his grandson with a spool of thread, the words that are uttered by the young boy function as signs (*fort*: "gone," *da*: "there") that give significance or meaning to the act of throwing the spool away and bringing it close. As signs, the words are reduced to the status of interpretations of the physical action of throwing and retrieving the spool of thread. But what if the words themselves, as voicings, also go out and come back; what if the words themselves, independent of which words they are, insist that by speaking there is the possibility of someone who is spoken to (dead or alive), who will be gathered up by the voice?

My thinking here depends on an interval between death and nonbeing. One can *be* dead just as one can *be* alive. So death is also form of being, a way to be. The dead call to the living, and the living attempt to send their voices to the dead. (Nonbeing, of course, is something else entirely, something that has, possibly, more to do with a kind of soundlessness. Is it true that there is something soundless about nonbeing, a soundlessness that death can only foreshadow?) My thinking also depends on the way words are not only vehicles of information or labels that fix the labeled in place but also gestures or even songs that allow a crooked, painful world, peopled by the living and the dead, to come into being.

Songs

In thinking about speech as song, and not just as information, I turn to the early ethnographic record of Inuit communities. The Danish explorer and ethnographer Knud Rasmussen collected a wide range of songs and poems from the Inuit he met in his travels across Arctic America in the 1920s. Orpingalik, the renowned Netsilik Inuit poet, shaman, and hunter, told Rasmussen that the songs he sang were his "comrades in solitude." In calling them comrades he foregrounds the being of a song, its life. He went on to say: "Songs are thoughts, sung out with the breath when people are moved by a great force, and *ordinary speech no longer suffices*. . . . [In those moments] we, who always think of ourselves as small, will feel still smaller. And we will fear to use words. But it will happen that the words we need will come of themselves. When the words we want to use shoot up of themselves—we get a new song."[23] Songs, for Orpingalik's people, as for other Inuit Rasmussen visited on his Fifth Thule Expedition of 1921–24, were not primarily a form of intentional or referential speech. They swell up when ordinary speech is no longer adequate to the task. Although songs are understood by Orpingalik to be thoughts, the words that give shape to those thoughts "shoot up of themselves." This means that songs, although they do refer to things in the world, are never straightforward acts of representation. They come from the world, and restore the Inuit to the being of the world, by placing them in relationship with a "comrade."[24] As Orpingalik said to Rasmussen, "All my being is song and I sing as I draw breath."[25]

During his visit to Orpingalik's camp in 1921, Rasmussen also recorded a song by Orpingalik's wife, Uvlunuaq. That year Uvlunuaq's son had fled to some remote hills after killing a hunting companion in a fit of rage. The actual words of her song express the shame she feels about her son's act and his subsequent flight. She says, for instance, that when she got the news of the killing and the flight, "Then I staggered / Like one unable to get a foothold." She asks,

Should I be ashamed
At the child I once carried
With me in my back-pouch
Because I heard of his flight
From the haunts of man?[26]

However, this song, a song that is "about" the loss of her son, actually opens not with the grief I have detailed above but with a remark about how she came to have a song to sing at all:

Eyaya-eya.
I recognize
A bit of song
And take it to me like a fellow being
Eyaya-eya.

The song continues in the vein I described above (calling her son's shame onto herself for not being as blameless as the blue sky), but already we understand that songs for Uvlunuaq are not ordinary speech. They are instead like fellow beings that she calls to her at moments when she stumbles and is unable to get a foothold. It seems that to sing a song—to be moved by a song—is to participate in, draw close to oneself, a being beyond oneself. The force of this song is to connect a mother to the being that also invests her fugitive son. As with Freud's story of his grandson, the words come and go, drawing being close.

In the 1960s an Italian ethnographer, Silvio Zavatti, working in Canada recorded a song about an Inuit caribou hunter who goes out hunting and unexpectedly discovers his child's body in the snow:

The Death of a Son

A man was leaving,
He was leaving alone,
He was walking in the cold,
He was walking in the wind,
He was going to the High Hill.
In the snow he saw something,
It was not a hare,
It was not a grouse,
It was something cold.
From the hands protruding from the snow,
From the feet protruding from the snow,
The hands had been chewed by the foxes,
The feet had been chewed by the wolves,
The father looked,
He looked without speaking.
He brushed the snow off the clothes,
He blew on the eyes,
He blew on the mouth;
He pressed his heart
His heart against the other's heart.
But the son remained cold,
Remained hard as a rock,
Still as ice,
And for three nights
The father could think no longer,
He lost his way,
He forgot the road,
He had no light,
No more light in his head.
Now the father sings,
He sings under the tent,
He sings with the Eskimo,
And together they all sing
They sing for the son.[27]

I want to say that when we form words in the face of devastating loss, we sing. That is, what we *say* when we say something in the face of loss, the noise and the gestures we make, I want to call song. The father described in the song above begins to sing when he can no longer think, when the road is forgotten, when there is no more light in his head . . . when his son is still as ice.

If the absent/dead threaten to recede into the stillness of ice or the shimmer of an underwater grave and thus dissolve the world as we know it (as an aside, this potential dissolution of a world is very clear in Freud's example where the child's world *is* the mother), how then do we describe the force of saying something? Do we call the absent/dead to us with every sounding of our voice? Is that partly what speech, even, perhaps especially, mundane, stuttering, unsure speech, is—a gathering of the spirits?

It's not like the spirits are necessarily kind or good, or that such calling is redemptive in our usual sense. It's hard to speak into the absence, and it's not as if such speech inoculates the speaker against the pain of living. Freud talks about his grandson gaining mastery of the situation, and in general Freud was interested in the way we pretend or delude ourselves into thinking death is something that happens to others, something that won't happen to us. But here I am interested in the way we create a world through speech/song that is not so much delusional as a courageous attempt to speak into the absence-that-is-death (that is, if we can call something essential to human life courageous). A mother calls out to her son—a man excommunicated for murder. A father sings in the face of his son's death by cold. The Inuit on the tape speak to their absent relatives. They say *something.*

In his work on creativity, Winnicott says that play is connected to the refusal to make a decision about what is real—is the teddy bear that shares my bed alive or not; is the toy train real or not?[28] Speaking to their relatives in sanatoria—relatives who may be dead or alive—the speakers on the tape also refuse such binary distinctions. Perhaps it's not so much mastery they achieve as a melancholic refusal to accede to the usual binaries—animate/inanimate, dead/alive, real/imagined, song/speech.

One of the speakers on the tape I found in the archive, Ittuq, a man from Arctic Bay, was less reticent than the others. "This is Ittuq," he says into the microphone and clears his throat. His voice is humble, thickened with age. As he speaks he picks up speed: "Speaking to my wife, E5-213: I think of you a lot. There are times when I don't think of you as much as I used to when you were first away. Last year just after you went away I nearly went out of my mind, but I'm now able to cope better. I get lonely for you very much." Then firmly, almost with a hint of defiance, he says, "I miss you very much." He pauses, and adds, "I love you very much." At this point there is a long silence interrupted only by the faint sounds of weeping. When he begins to speak again, he struggles with the words, his voice rising in pitch, as if it might split. "I worry a lot, though. I don't know what else to say at the moment so I'm just going to say bye for now."

Ittuq says more than most of those who spoke into the tape recorder the nurse had brought with her.[29] But still he asserts, as so many of the speakers did, that "I don't know what else to say at the moment." What news does it make sense to give? What is there to be said? Ittuq wouldn't have known definitively whether his words would reach his wife alive. But in the act of speaking, in the act of sending his words into the absence-that-is-death, he calls a world into being, a world to which she belongs—dead or alive.

Ittuq says, "I nearly went out of my mind." Leah Idlout says, "I had never felt so alone before." The forms of address I am describing—this speech recorded on a tape that is sent out into the absence—occurs in the context of the particular violence of the attempts by the Canadian state to care for the Inuit. My reflections in this essay, on instances when saying something is more important than what is said, are obviously not meant to discount the violence that speech, in its semantic specificity, can enact.

For instance, Audra Simpson has called our attention to the experience common to indigenous communities, "of being defined as some thing, 'a problem,' that needed to be dealt with," as well as to the harrowing experience of "being defined solely in those terms."[30] Simpson challenges us to think again about what it might mean and feel like for indigenous people to be continually and insistently interpellated as a problem.

The single-minded focus on making Inuit well meant that the northern administrators couldn't hear the lament that was pouring out of Inuit communities. The "problem" that Inuit communities represented lay in their terrible (and very un-Canadian) death rates. Resolving that problem meant keeping Inuit alive at all costs. For the Inuit, it was rarely a question of life at all costs. This is partly because being alive and being in community are inextricably linked.[31] It is also partly because, as I tease out in the next section, we are already all in some sense dead, and the dead can be called and can call the living. For many Inuit, then, the problem was more how to live *and die* in the company of those they loved.

Being Already Dead

Stories of death seem to form the tissue of life, of land, in the arctic communities I have come to know. Inuit, children even, narrate death as part of the everyday—the land is marked by death, as are their lives. In Pangnirtung: "On the third blue hill, the bluest, over there, is where my grandfather, a shaman, died in a wrestling duel." Or, in Iqaluit, pointing at the residence for the Nunavut Arctic College, "That's the window of the room where my friend committed suicide." And as we drive through town, "That's the place where Eli's car went off the road, that's where the little girl was hit by the sewage truck." Death is woven into the modern arctic landscape of tundra and rock, metal and glass. It seems to actually constitute the habitable world, to somehow emplace the world instead of marking its limit.

Death is also something that Inuit, at least before moving into fixed settlements, prepared for assiduously. Beginning in early childhood, Inuit were taught to imagine the deaths of their parents and siblings. Jean L. Briggs, an ethnographer who conducted fieldwork in the 1960s in one of the last outpost camps near the settlement of Pangnirtung, describes the way Inuit children are trained from a very young age to recognize the uncertainty of life and the ever-present possibility of death. A three-year-old child whose father is out hunting is teased incessantly with questions like, "Where is your father? You think he's coming back to you? How do you know? What makes you think he's coming back?"[32]

I know this form of instruction intimately. One summer while I was living in Iqaluit, my brother, who was teaching at the local high school, went on a kayaking trip to Greenland with some friends and took my younger teenage brother along. I had a deep sense of foreboding. Neither of them had ever been on a kayaking trip before, and now they planned to paddle through arctic waters in heavily loaded boats, dealing with unfamiliar tides and wind. Tipping meant nearly certain death. The elder of my two brothers said I worried too much. Toward the end of their ten-day trip, an Inuit friend called me. "They're not back yet?" she exclaimed. "I thought they were supposed to be back yesterday." Then after a pause, "Aren't you worried about them?" I admitted that I was. "Don't you keep picturing them under the water looking up at you, saying 'Help! Help!'?" She paused, and continued, "Because I do." I was being taught to imagine the death of my brothers, to prepare for it, by visualizing them under the water, their voices lost in the foam and fury of an unrelenting sea.

Inuit youth I knew communicated with the dead through their dreams, sometimes in amusing ways (agreeing to meet their friends to smoke a last joint, getting advice on boyfriends) and sometimes in frightening ways. Many spoke of being called by their dead friends and relatives who have committed suicide to be with them in an afterworld. These calls can come through dreams, in visions, or as a voice in your head. A teenage girl told me: "I had this dream after my cousin killed herself—like a month later or two—I had a dream I was in this dark place and there was a couple of people. They were like, 'Ilisapi, help me!'" She continues, "You know those bushes, but they're not bushes? They're like roses but no rose on them. They're like circles going around, and there's these thorn things, like spiky things?"

"That was on Jesus's head supposedly?"

"Yup. They were all over, all tangled up. So my cousin and this other person . . . were hiding behind those things, or trapped, or *something.*

They were like, 'Ilisapi, help me, help me please, get me outta here!' And there was this deep scary voice, laughing, freakily. And they kept saying, 'Help me, Ilisapi!' And after, I dunno, this freaky voice said, 'Ilisapi, kill yourself, your cousin did.'"

Many of the teenagers I knew had already chosen where they wanted to be buried when they died (often near the camps of their ancestors). Sometimes they seemed to be cavalier about death, but it wasn't that at all. Once, out camping on the land, I got to know a young man, Eli,[33] who had recently been released from prison in southern Ontario. The main activity of the camp was beluga hunting, but we also went swimming in the nearby lakes—steeling ourselves against the numbing coldness that makes your temples throb. On our way to the lakes we climbed by an old camping site of his family. Eli pointed out the misshapen circles of rocks, almost hidden by grass and lichen, that were the tent rings of his grandparents. He showed us the rock wall beside the camp that he and his brother used to try to climb. There were bits of debris scattered around from the old camp, rusted metal mattress springs, bits of a bucket, and some old gasoline cans. In the crevasse nearby were a series of wooden coffins with stones piled around: his ancestors. We skirted around them, climbing up toward the lake for a swim. We talked a lot about his time in prison and the fact that he never got to say goodbye to his grandfather who died while he was down South.

"We're just people," he explained later, after recounting several terrifying stories about his run-ins with Hells Angels gang members in prison.

"Weren't you scared?" I asked.

"No," he replied, as if that were a slightly ridiculous suggestion.

"Well, *I* would have been scared," I insisted.

"No, I wasn't scared. We're just people." He explained this to me patiently, as if it's something he knew and I didn't. "We're human. So we gotta die sometime. Nobody lives forever."

Eli's words remind me of the incantation to be spoken when suddenly in mortal danger that a man from Iglulik, Padloq, told Rasmussen in the 1920s:

> See, great earth
> These heaps
> Of pale bone in the wind!
> They crumble in the air
> Of the wide world
> In the wide world's air
> Pale, wind-dried bones
> Decaying in the air![34]

It seems that in order to live, to avoid death this time around, we need to recognize that we are just people—pale, wind-dried bones. We need to recognize that we are already, in some sense, dead.

A central part of the argument in my book *Life beside Itself* (2014) has to do with the way Inuit are repeatedly being interpellated into the subject position of a problematic statistic. To give just an intimation of this argument, think about the Inuit buried in unmarked graves during the tuberculosis epidemic. What other burial does a person who has become only a statistic in the eyes of the state require? Or consider the story of Kaujaq, whose tubercular body is unloaded from a train and promptly disappears from the memory and records of those caring for her.[35] Keeping Inuit alive improved Canada's northern death rates. Once they were dead they were no longer useful to the state.

I don't think the Inuit speaking into the recorders were first and foremost assigning their listeners an identity; to listen to their voices takes us somewhere else. So here I am also trying to think about the "call" that is at the heart of our notion of interpellation in its less violent aspect. I am interested, then, in the relationship between being and calling, or the way *saying* something—calling out to someone into the absence-that-is-also-death—allows the other to be: my interest is in calling and being rather than interpellation and identity.

What I am proposing here and in *Life beside Itself* is not a novel way of understanding speech. Ernst Cassirer argued that, in fact, "in all mythical cosmogonies, as far back as they can be traced" the word has "a sort of primary force, in which all being and doing originate."[36] In anthropology, with our interest in culture figured as text, we have perhaps moved toward a somewhat limiting notion of speech as discourse—a concern with how words wound and what kinds of information they convey, what kind of violence they enact. Often, in anthropology, when we talk about this way of understanding speech (speech as song, or the song of speech), we tend to relegate it to a domain of speech that should be kept separate from our more dominant communicative rationalities. For instance, Bronislaw Malinowski described phatic language as "a flow of language, purposeless expressions of preference or aversion, accounts of irrelevant happenings, comments on what is perfectly obvious . . . a type of speech in which ties of union are created by the mere exchange of words."[37] This notion is very close to what I am trying to describe in this article. It's just that I want to think about these phatic properties as inhering in our speech more generally (not simply as "purposeless expressions"), and I also want to think about such "ties of union" thus created as somehow constitutive of being humanly alive.

In its simplest sense, I take "song" as an invocation that depends less on the semantic meaning of words, or even the existence of words per se, and more on voice as a kind of gesture. I want, thus, to pay attention to those moments when it matters less *what* is being said than that *something* is being said—or, more precisely, that someone, an Other, is speaking, or even singing.

Recently I read, for the first time, an interview with Roland Barthes where he specifically alludes to Malinowski's notion of phatic speech. He gives the example of someone saying, "Hello, hello, can you hear me?" and suggests that, although such utterances may seem unassuming, they are actually "discreetly dramatic" and that we should think of such acts of speech as "appeals, modulations, should I say, thinking of birds: songs?—through which a body seeks another body."[38]

Thinking in this way about the "song of speech" also brings to mind the sounds of grunting that Inuit adults make to children (and sometimes to anthropologists) as an expression of profound and playful love. Sometimes words are grunted like "Ajunnni!" Sometimes just a grunt is voiced. Other times, in a form of speech called *aqaq*, whole strings of phrases are repeated over and over in a tender, even silly voice. An adult will have a special way of talking, and a particular string words that he or she repeats over and over, to single out and recognize a specific child.[39]

So in thinking through the song of speech I am also trying to delineate a possible mode of anthropological listening[40]—a mode that is more like listening to music than deciphering a code. Italo Calvino in his short story "A King Listens" beautifully draws out these two modes of listening. The first mode is that of a paranoid king, paralyzed by the fear that someone/something will usurp his power. "You" listen to every sound as if it might be a sign of a coming insurrection. Any sound that deviates from the usual is suspect; every voice that speaks has ulterior motives. Calvino writes the story in the second person, as if you, the reader, were the king. He writes: "From every shard of sound you continue to gather signals, information, clues, as if in this city all those who play or sing or put on disks wanted only to transmit precise, unequivocal messages to you."[41] The second mode of listening is that of listening to music. The king is surprised to hear a voice singing in the castle, a voice that is neither asking anything of him nor threatening him. "You," the king, are stunned. It's as if you don't know how to listen to the voice. Calvino writes, "Now you ask yourself what listening used to mean to you, when you listened to music for the sole pleasure of penetrating the design of the notes."[42] What might it mean as an anthropologist to listen to speech as we might listen to song? What might we hear that we don't already?[43] Obviously speech often conveys vital information, and decoding that information, understanding it, using it, is our first task. But there are moments when the fact that speech is always also voice, also sounds that are sent out into a gap, becomes of vital importance, moments when in listening we need to concentrate on the vocal and ignore the semantic.[44]

The fact that the Inuit speaking into the recorders to their family members in hospital didn't know what to say, that words themselves failed them, pushes us to consider speech also as voice—voice because its primary function is not intelligibility but sound as it communicates, as it moves between and ties people together. And part of what I am suggesting is that, in moving between us, voice can also animate us, or allows us the space to be whatever it is that we are.

I'll end with this thought: could this way of thinking give a new inflection to what we mean by the other in politics and anthropology? That is, is there a parallel between the absent/dead and the other, insofar as the danger is that the other will recede into soundlessness? If so, then speaking—*saying* something—allows the other to *be*, dead or alive. I wonder also about rethinking politics through our ability to pause before our rush to distill or communicate meaning—to hear the voice also as music and not just as the vehicle of information. Could such a pause present a moment in which we might hear something else, something that might enliven us to another way of conceiving of life, politics, and our relation to the other?

Notes

1. Freud, *Beyond the Pleasure Principle*, 13–14.
2. Winnicott, *Playing and Reality*, 29.
3. Cockman, "Interview with Dr. Austin Peer."
4. Quoted in Grygier, *A Long Way from Home*, 86.
5. Ibid., 98.
6. Tester, McNicoll, and Irniq, "Writing for Our Lives," 131.
7. Grygier, *A Long Way from Home*, 115.
8. Yatsushiro, a Japanese American who grew up in Hawaii, was first exposed to anthropology as an internee at Poston, an internment camp for Japanese Americans where he was interned during World War II. His first job after graduating from Cornell University with a degree in anthropology was at McGill, where he turned his attentions from his work on the "governing of men" within the internment camps to the Inuit. His research, funded by Canada's Department of Northern Affairs, concerned the Inuit transition to wage employment. In 2005 Nelson Graburn and I traveled to Hawaii together and stayed with Yatsushiro in his apartment, where he shared with us the images, films, and audiotapes he had collected in those years.
9. Name has been changed.
10. Canadian Broadcasting Corporation, "Interview with Bryan Pearson."
11. Idlout, "Little Arctic Tern."
12. Ibid., 26.
13. D'Argencourt, "*C. D. Howe*," 228.
14. Ibid., 226.
15. McGrath, "Monster Figures."

16. But survival in Inuit stories and lives, as in our own, is rarely innocent, rarely merely a matter of living instead of dying. Survival often gestures toward an "other" death: the death of the one (or many) who died instead of you, in your place, or because of you.

17. Cockman, "Interview with Dr. Austin Peer."

18. Petrovich, "Interview with Dr. Hugo Ewart."

19. Canadian Broadcasting Corporation, *Inuit Tuberculosis Footage.*

20. Eastern Arctic Patrol, "Messages to Patients in Mountain San."

21. I have not been able to find a copy of this recording, only a transcription in a memo sent from one arctic administrator (Ben Sivertz) to another (R. A. J. Phillips) on 25 October 1956.

22. Downie, "Interview with Martha Michaels."

23. Quoted in Rasmussen, *Netsilik Eskimos*, 321; emphasis added.

24. This notion of the song as a "comrade" or "being" resonates, as one anonymous reviewer helpfully pointed out, with long-standing Western conceptions of the artistic text as in some sense alive or, as many contemporary authors suggest, "as creatures to be sought after, enticed, and perhaps trapped" (Tomlinson, *Authors on Writing*, 78).

25. Ibid., 16.

26. Quoted in Rasmussen, *Netsilik Eskimos*, 16–17.

27. Quoted in Petrone, *Northern Voices,* 36–37.

28. Winnicott, *Playing and Reality.*

29. I have written briefly about Ittuq (and his son Peutagok) before, but I have not left off thinking about them (see Stevenson, *Life beside Itself*). What I write here is an attempt to come to terms with the way that Ittuq's words can be thought of as song in the Inuit sense, and how they can be thought of as invoking or calling another person into being.

30. Simpson, "Commentary," 376.

31. In fact, by the 1960s some Inuit had begun using the Inuktitut word *qivituk* to translate the concept of suicide. *Qivituk*, however, connotes a kind of self-detachment from one's community. Graburn, "Eskimo Law."

32. Briggs, *Inuit Morality Play.*

33. Name has been changed.

34. Rasmussen and Lowenstein, *Eskimo Poems*, 95.

35. Stevenson, "Psychic Life of Biopolitics."

36. Cassirer, *Language and Myth*, 45.

37. Malinowski, "Problem of Meaning," 314–15.

38. Barthes, *Grain of the Voice*, 4–5.

39. This is a way of thinking about speech that, as one anonymous reviewer noted, is less interested in "how sounds and words come into discursive alignment with socially identifiable types of persons" or "how utterances index typifiable speaking personae" and more about the way words, like Barthes's birdsong, seek out the body and being of another. It's about how words body forth.

40. Stevenson, *Life beside Itself.*

41. Calvino, "A King Listens," 51.

42. Ibid., 52.

43. An anonymous reviewer formulated this as the question of "how we are to be with the words of others," a formulation I appreciate a lot.

44. Cavarero, *For More than One Voice.*

References

Barthes, Roland. 1986. *The Grain of the Voice: Interviews 1962–1980*. Translated by Linda Coverdale. New York: Hill and Wang.

Briggs, Jean L. 1998. *Inuit Morality Play: The Emotional Education of a Three-Year-Old*. New Haven, CT: Yale University Press.

Calvino, Italo. 1988. "A King Listens." In *Under the Jaguar Sun*, translated by William Weaver, 31–64. San Diego: Harcourt Brace Jovanovich.

Canadian Broadcasting Corporation. 1956. *Inuit Tuberculosis Footage* (television broadcast). 19 August. Mag 56-08-19. Canadian Broadcast Corporation Television Archives, Toronto.

Canadian Broadcasting Corporation. 1973. "Interview with Bryan Pearson." *Weekend* (television broadcast). 4 April. 730408-6. Canadian Broadcasting Corporation Radio Archives, Toronto.

Cassirer, Ernst. 1946. *Language and Myth*. Translated by Susanne K. Langer. New York: Dover.

Cavarero, Adriana. 2005. *For More than One Voice: Toward a Philosophy of Vocal Expression*. Stanford, CA: Stanford University Press.

Cockman, Bill. 1959. "Interview with Dr. Austin Peer." *Assignment* (radio broadcast). Canadian Broadcast Corporation Radio. 15 May. CBC Digital Archives. www.cbc.ca/archives/entry/inuit-go-south-for-tuberculosis-treatment.

D'Argencourt, Leah Idlout. 1988. "*C. D. Howe*." In *Northern Voices: Inuit Writing in English*, edited by Penny Petrone, 225–34. Toronto: University of Toronto Press.

Downie, Peter. 1989. "Interview with Martha Michaels." *Midday* (television broadcast). Canadian Broadcasting Corporation. 30 January. www.cbc.ca/archives/entry/tuberculosis-tb-treatment-in-south-takes-inuit-from-their-families.

Eastern Arctic Patrol. 1961. "Messages to Patients in Mountain San." Domain CMH, James Sylvia, Series: Inuit patients, box 1. Archives of Hamilton Health Sciences and Faculty of Health Science at McMaster University, Hamilton, ON.

Freud, Sigmund. 1975. *Beyond the Pleasure Principle*. Translated by James Strachey. New York: Norton.

Graburn, Nelson. 1969. "Eskimo Law in Light of Self- and Group-Interest." *Law and Society Review* 4, no. 1: 45–60.

Grygier, Pat Sandiford. 1994. *A Long Way from Home: The Tuberculosis Epidemic among the Inuit*. Montreal: McGill-Queen's University Press.

Idlout, Leah. 1980. "The Little Arctic Tern, the Big Polar Bear." In *Paper Stays Put: A Collection of Inuit Writing*, edited by Gedalof Robin, 21–26. Edmonton: Hurtig.

Malinowski, Bronislaw. 1923. "The Problem of Meaning in Primitive Languages." In *The Meaning of Meaning: A Study of the Influence of Language upon Thought and of the Science of Symbolism*. Supplement I, edited by C. K. Ogden and I. A. Richards, 296–336. London: Kegan Paul, Tench, Trübner.

McGrath, Robin. 1988. "Monster Figures and Unhappy Endings in Inuit Literature." *Canadian Journal of Native Education* 15, no. 1: 51–58.

Petrone, Penny. 1988. *Northern Voices: Inuit Writing in English*. Toronto: University of Toronto Press.

Petrovich, Curt. 1989. "Interview with Dr. Hugo Ewart." *North by Northwest* (radio broadcast). Canadian Broadcasting Corporation. 13 January. Northern Service Fonds, N-1995-001:0176. NWT Archives, Yellowknife.

Rasmussen, Knud. 1931. *The Netsilik Eskimos: Social Life and Spiritual Culture*. Copenhagen: Gyldendalske Boghandel, Nordisk Forlag.

Rasmussen, Knud, and Tom Lowenstein. 1973. *Eskimo Poems from Canada and Greenland*. Pittsburgh: University of Pittsburgh Press.

Simpson, Audra. 2008. "Commentary: The 'Problem' of Mental Health in Native North America: Liberalism, Multiculturalism, and the (Non)Efficacy of Tears." *Ethos* 36, no. 3: 376–79.

Sivertz, Ben. 1956. Memo to R. A. J. Phillips. RG85 1473 251-1 (5). Library and Archives Canada, Ottawa.

Stevenson, Lisa. 2012. "The Psychic Life of Biopolitics: Survival, Cooperation, and Inuit Community." *American Ethnologist* 39, no. 3: 592–613.

Stevenson, Lisa. 2014. *Life beside Itself: Imagining Care in the Canadian Arctic*. Berkeley: University of California Press.

Tester, Frank James, Paule McNicoll, and Peter Irniq. 2001. "Writing for Our Lives: The Language of Homesickness, Self-Esteem and the Inuit TB 'Epidemic.'" *Études Inuit Studies* 25, nos. 1–2: 121–40.

Tomlinson, Barbara. 2005. *Authors on Writing: Metaphors and Intellectual Labor*. New York: Palgrave Macmillan.

Winnicott, D. W. 2005. *Playing and Reality*. London: Routledge.

In-durable Sociality

Precarious Life in Common and the Temporal Boundaries of the Social

Zoë H. Wool

On a fall afternoon in 2007, more than a year after Jake had been medically evacuated from Iraq to the US military's iconic Walter Reed Army Medical Center in Washington, DC, he and I sat perched on a seasonal grocery store display of pumpkins and haystacks in front of a nearby mall, talking and waiting for the pain in his leg to subside. Jake reflected on his faltering new marriage to his newly pregnant wife, now on bed rest back home in South Carolina, and his as yet unsuccessful attempts to convince doctors to amputate his reconstructed but still-useless leg. Weary and frustrated, he said Walter Reed is the place where "you have to wait around before you can even begin picking up the pieces." The "pieces" Jake referred to were the fragmented stuff of an aspirationally ordinary American life, signaled in this context by marriage more than anything else. And this was inextricable from the fragmented stuff of his body—his shattered foot, his torn and sutured and incised flesh, the damaged gray matter of his brain. Through the image of a shattered whole, he evokes both a world and a body blown apart and indexes the waiting that fills the days at Walter Reed, a waiting that feels to him like a doing nothing that has become everything.[1] Waiting, of course, can be an ethical, or even reparative, practice.[2] Recall the familiar gendered trope of the lover who longingly waits for her soldier's return. But for Jake, waiting registers as nonaction. Not a waiting *for*, but a waiting *around*. In this moment, the essential difference is that waiting for is productively attached to an other and a future legible within heteronormative regimes of sociality; waiting around just uselessly circles a relentless present, a negative evocation of the temporalities of disability that refuse the productive organization

Social Text 130 · Vol. 35, No. 1 · March 2017
DOI 10.1215/01642472-3728008 © 2017 Duke University Press

of lifetimes essential to heteronormative and capitalist fantasies of the good life.[3]

This ethnographic situation rhymes with its broader historical one in which, in the United States in particular, normative fantasies of the good life are frayed, hard to grasp, and increasingly costly in the attempt, and yet investment in them and aspiration for them remain a central force that pushes people's lives along, even as they seem to go nowhere.[4] This is, after all, how many people, including Jake, end up in the army in these days of the all-volunteer force and GI Bill benefits.[5] With its steady pay, education and health benefits, and touted opportunities for employment, soldiers are more likely to have seen enlistment as an alternative to the perils of low-wage or no work than as a chance to fulfill some patriotic destiny. And so, while there is much in the experiences I present below that is specifically conditioned by America's war in Iraq in the decade following 9/11, there is also a good deal that speaks to the problems of aspiration, desperation, and the difficulties of enduring life in the midst of a profound uncertainty that both emanates from and registers in the body itself.

This stuckness in a difficult and undesirable present that does not seem to advance toward the future is the temporality of endurance, a temporality Elizabeth Povinelli has identified with those daily experiences of "suffering and dying . . . that are chronic and cruddy," unfolding in the social tense of the durative present, never rising to the level of the event.[6] This is akin to what Lauren Berlant has thought through the "impasse," emphasizing affective modes of sheltering in place while waiting for a new genre of social life to emerge.[7] Endurance is not the work of overcoming adversity, of moving on or moving elsewhere, but the practices of making do in a protracted moment of dire and even life-threatening uncertainty that seems so relentless it becomes ordinary. The questions I pose about it here concern the modes of intimate sociality that adhere in such a moment. Attending ethnographically to this fragmented and overwhelming present-out-of-time at Walter Reed, we encounter attachments and modes of solitude that both sustain and imperil existence. While sometimes gesturing toward the future, Jake and others at Walter Reed were often overcome by the sense that they were doing nothing but waiting, and waiting for nothing. In response to this sense of nothing, I ask, what broader logics of the social govern this space such that Jake can posit its modes of intimacy, violence, care, and obligation as something other than the living of life, as waiting around? And what analytic interventions might we pose as critical thinkers of the social to allow all this to register as something more?

I am concerned with the situated particularities of the group of injured soldiers I knew at Walter Reed. But I am also concerned with how these particularities might push us to refocus our thinking about the lived experiences of biosocial precarity. In seeing soldiers as exemplary subjects for thinking sociality, I am reminded that Michel Foucault found soldiers exemplary subjects of disciplinary power and also turned to soldier sociality as a productive example ready at hand when reflecting on relational modes that challenge normative arrangements of sex and love.[8] Here I move between the contours of daily experience for injured soldiers at Walter Reed and a broader consideration of how we might theorize the contours and temporalities of sociality, solitude, life, and its limits in such precarious spaces and moments. In doing so, I home in on a mode of sociality I term *in-durable*, one that may be illegible to social theory that takes its objects from those things that constitute normative arrangements of life, or the events that change them,[9] or that contain a "transformative potential of becoming."[10]

When it does occur, attention to the sociality of suffering bodies is sometimes explained, or justified, by the suggestion that such socialities might be politically transformative, that their precarious present is on the verge of the future, part of the emergence of "a people yet to come." But, echoing recent work in other zones of life configured between being and not being,[11] my work with soldiers like Jake compels me to attend to something else, a way of being that is shared and that is more *in* the verge than *on* it: in a zone of life seemingly hostile to stabilizing social forms, to the enduring temporality of the social, where questions of emergence may be secondary to practices of being with others between emergence and collapse. Here, the focus is not on the event, the transformative emergence of a new relational mode or otherwise world, but on the moment, the daily experience of difficult and deeply uncertain life that is circumscribed within a present that seems to go nowhere.

In-durable Sociality in the Shadow of Conjugal Couplehood

Jake stayed at Walter Reed for about three years, undergoing the amputation of his lower leg after about a year and a half. While his stay was longer than most (the average was about fourteen months), it wasn't all that unusual. Delayed amputations like his, the result of repeated surgical and rehabilitative failures to restore sufficient function (though sufficient to what was a topic of careful consideration among soldiers), were increasingly common. There are a good many American soldiers "like Jake," many thousands, depending on how you want to count them. As of the time he finally left Walter Reed—three years, more than twenty surgeries, one marriage, one separation, one amputation, and two children after being blown up by an improvised explosive device (IED) in Iraq—Jake could be counted as one of roughly 45,500 who had been medevaced out of Iraq, one of 1,200 who had partial or total limb amputations, and one of

7,800 who had come through Walter Reed, nearly all with a family member who rushed to their side.[12] Soldiers might spend years living within Walter Reed's gates, most often in a room in the on-post Mologne House hotel or the nonprofit communal family-home-style Fisher House, where my research was based. They shared their room with a family member—a wife or girlfriend, a cousin or a brother—helping constitute each soldier as an individuated family man. The routines and roles of military life were largely absent, and institutional life increasingly gave way to forms of civilian anonymity that were cultivated within it.

In 2007 Walter Reed was populated by a few hundred soldiers, most of them grievously injured in Iraq, blown up by IEDs. Most of them were young men, and almost all of them had a wife or girlfriend or a parent or sibling or cousin or friend who came and was menially compensated to live with them as what was called a nonmedical attendant while efforts were made to remake the violences of war into the stuff of unmarked American life.[13] Unlike civilian Americans who require long-term rehabilitation, soldiers like Jake have a massive health care apparatus and surfeit of public, private, and political will and resources to support them. They also find themselves hailed by narratives of heroism, trauma, and recovery that function as a proxy for the nation's own success, failure, triumph, or decline, urging them into the comforting time line of a crisis overcome, a promising myth of social and biomedical repair. The sometimes prosthetic production of normative and normatively gendered bodily forms is a key feature of biomedicalized regimes of recovery elsewhere in the United States, as critical work on mastectomy has made clear.[14] The body of the injured soldier is similarly rendered as a figure that plays out public anxieties about gendered embodiment, debility, and sexuality. But more than the body of the woman with cancer, the body of the injured soldier becomes a kind of avatar of the nation itself, both in its form and function and in the arrangements of life it entails.

Historians have been particularly apt at demonstrating the ways this figure is instrumental to the production of various regimes of the social.[15] The question of to what social form soldiers will be disbursed when they are no longer soldiers, particularly after injury, has always exerted some sort of pressure on the institutions that were obligated to them when they were. The earliest pension and welfare system in the United States, for example, was the one created for Revolutionary War soldiers in 1818, which was expanded for Civil War soldiers in 1865 in part to create group homes for disabled veterans.[16] When the country was preparing for the return of World War I soldiers, it created an insurance scheme, rather than a pension, aimed largely at ensuring the return of fighting men, both injured and not, to the workforce and to the ideal domestic configuration of male-headed single-family households tended by nonworking wives and mothers.[17]

Thus the whiteness, maleness, and re/productive fitness of the veteran body has long been embedded in the biopolitics of veteran care. The iterations of the GI Bill that began in 1944 have been organized around benefits like education, housing, and medical care, aimed at bringing waves of returning soldiers productively back into the social fold.

These efforts at governing and securing the futures of soldiers have met with mixed success, occasionally giving rise to bastard social forms. There was the Bonus Army of 1932: thousands of World War I veterans who marched to Washington, DC, set up an encampment near the Capitol, and vowed to remain until they were given the compensation they had been promised. For two months a kind of otherwise community flourished, with provisions shared and color lines broken by common need, common cause, and common experiences of wartime army life that left a lingering legacy of government "fear of veteran activism."[18] Fred Zinnemann's 1950 film *The Men* stages the tension between the normative domestic world into which injured soldiers ought to return, and the queer crip homosociality (still heterosexual, though not heteronormative) of the men on the veterans' hospital's wards that threatens it. It is this homosociality, rather than the devotion of his fiancée, that offers Ken, the film's protagonist (played by Marlon Brando), the forms of intimacy and camaraderie he finds most nourishing and vital.[19] And it was largely out of the failures of the Veterans Administration (VA) to help Vietnam veterans "readjust" to normative social forms of civilian life that the hybrid politico-therapeutic form of the rap group arose, not only creating sustaining forms of veteran homosociality that counterbalanced normative forms but also, in so doing, helping to feed the veteran antiwar movement consolidated by the organization Vietnam Veterans against the War.[20]

Such forms of potentially long-lasting, oppositional, and transformative collectivity did not take root at Walter Reed. Instead, Walter Reed was an uncanny space that attempted to replicate the comforts of home while being virtually overrun with celebrities, politicians, volunteers, and reporters who claimed injured soldiers as willing national sacrifices. In this strange space where the ordinary and extraordinary collided, there were the in-durable socialities of the present and an impossibly narrow horizon of the future that was supposed to be secured by the antipolitical and love-bound form of conjugal couplehood from which few fugitive routes to the future escaped.[21] *In-durable sociality* is the inelegant name I give to a way of being with others based in part on a common need for endurance but that is not itself enduring, a way of being in common that is based on the hardness (*dureté*) of life—both its difficulty and its explicit materiality—but that is also conditioned by the temporal limits of that togetherness: the awareness of many, finite durations, rather than the possibility of a single shared one (*the* duration). The inspiration for thinking of these modes of sociality at Walter Reed in terms of the French and English cognates of duration, endurance, and *dureté* comes from my slightly ironic rethinking of the Paul Éluard quotation that is the epitaph of Michael Lambek's *Weight of the Past*, "le dur désir de durer," roughly translated as "the difficult desire to endure."[22] Beyond the difficulty of endurance, the ambiguous syntax also points us to the difficulty of this desire itself, suggesting the fundamental ambivalence of attachments that keep you living in a present you want to leave behind. At Walter Reed people knew that this mode of life would not last, and indeed they hoped it would not last long. After all, in the best of all possible worlds, they will be able to leave Walter Reed and its sociality tomorrow. But, despite their apparent thinness and fragility, the social attachments that adhere in this moment are essential to the practices of endurance, of waiting out the present, out of which daily life at Walter Reed is largely made: in-durability is a quality of the social attachments that help sustain life in a finite and protracted present that is difficult to endure.

In-durable sociality names the attachments Jake had with other injured soldiers, the attachments that could seem so essential but also feel to him like nothing when overshadowed by the normative form of conjugal couplehood that he, and so many others, tended to hang his future on. As opposed to these ways of living, precariously, in common, with others, for a while, the normative arrangement of conjugal couplehood seemed best, the most reliable for the future, even if it was unstable in the present. While it has long informed rehabilitative practices and redemptive national desires that aim to enfold injured soldiers within normative civilian life after war, the shift in emphasis from wage earning to conjugal couplehood as offering the most whole, hopeful, and long-lasting future is new.[23] It is hard to overestimate the tenacity of this form in the American military context, where institutional investments in making the military more "family friendly"—where the "family" form imagined was only the heteronationally normative one—was essential to transitioning to an all-volunteer force after the end of the draft in 1973. This form continues to be considered central to the functioning of the force and, in new ways, to the care of injured soldiers and veterans, even as it becomes increasingly clear that such a limited set does not begin to capture the number or arrangement of intimacies out of which soldier and veteran lives are maintained, or the many ways that such limited intimacies can be hazardous. Nevertheless, the supposed stability of that normative life lingered out on the horizon of rehabilitation at Walter Reed, an imagined future in which the body and mind were no trouble at all and where the social form of a heteronational nuclear family would both rely on and shore up the formerly wounded soldier at its center.

Attempting to cultivate this arrangement in the present was exhausting. Sometimes it seemed to work. Many marriages faltered and some failed at and after Walter Reed, though every so often one would be consolidated through the pressures and practices of enduring its present. Occasionally people even met and fell in love there: a soldier whose civilian "pen pal" came to visit him and then became his wife, another who went on to marry a graduate student interning there. But sometimes these attempts undermined the stability of the lives they were supposed to support, as when wives or girlfriends hit, shoved, or betrayed soldiers.[24]

Soldiers were not institutionally bound to one another, but they might see one another every day in brief increments crossing paths in the hospital's rehab spaces or punctuating empty hours in their rooms by taking smoke breaks in common spaces outside. Skipping over the incremental steps of getting to know one another in favor of profound identification and affiliation, they would swap details that became relevant in the moment: comparing the present shakiness of a body to the previously honed stability of a sniper's concentration; recounting the effects and side effects of narcotic painkillers, antibiotics, sleep and psych meds, and erectile dysfunction drugs; weighing the labors and maintenance of an amputated leg against the pain of a dysfunctional one. In this way they made deep friendships missing the superficial layers of acquaintance, an intimate bond with someone whose name you might not know.

That they shared seemingly extraordinary things in common was the core of their vital and in-durable attachments to each other. This commonness did not constitute a community, but it was a kind of shared world, a world of fragments, a world without a future, a world whose necessity was bound to the particularities and intensities of a present, which was perforated by, and always ready to break toward, a time after now that never seemed to come.

Jake's practice of waiting was like this, too. He and Manny, another injured soldier, were practically inseparable when they both lived at the Fisher House. They would go to the mall together, work on cars in the parking lot together, watch TV together, keep each other going just by being side-by-side. They plotted a future together and talked about opening a garage in South Carolina—Jake even scoped out a location one weekend on leave. But this is not a future that will come to pass. It matters as an imagined future, not an actual one. It matters as part of a shared present, not as a shared future. And when there is a special workshop for injured soldiers who want to start their own businesses, neither Jake nor Manny attends.

When Manny plans a visit home to California, Jake is worried about how he'll spend his time. He's worried about getting depressed and tells me that if he stops shaving, I will know he is not doing very well. But despite days' worth of stubble, despite forest fires that suddenly erupt in Manny's California hometown, the two of them are not in touch. Then, back at the Fisher House, they are inseparable once again, living on in each other's company day after day. But once Jake's wife and Manny's mother must leave Walter Reed, and Jake and Manny each move into the Abrams Hall barracks for single soldiers, they don't see each other for days on end. Text messages are considered and often go unsent. It is again as if Manny is across the country rather than across the courtyard. It is as though the pace of life is too much, too fast, too soon, and relationships pounded out in this rhythm appear thick and prove brittle.

In-durable sociality can become a cause for concern, including concern about what forms of life will emerge after Walter Reed. This is especially the case when, as would prove to be true for Jake, there is no obvious civilian life or robust domestic arrangement to return to and no way of continuing the army life soldiers had come to know.

In the contemporary American public imaginary, ideas about the afterlives of soldiers are shadowed by the war-crazed and war-broken veteran figures of the Vietnam War era. And both public and more proximate concerns about what soldiers like Jake will be are haunted by specters of suicide, homicide, and other forms of violence that seem to stick to them. These are often poised between the deathboundedness of injured soldiers and the redemptive possibility that their bodies might become stabilized through normative social forms, especially through heteronational domesticity, that configuration of life that is the apotheosis of successful rehabilitation.[25] At Walter Reed, these concerns for life in the future are complicated by concerns for life in the present. In-durable sociality, after all, may make life bearable, but it is made of unreliable stuff. The fantasy of clear—though only ever ideal—alignments between solitude and social death, independence and the capacity for self-founding social life, between physical proximity and bodily care and social attachment becomes untenable at Walter Reed. Amid this precarity of both social and biological life, the kinds of sociality and solitude that sustain life and those that represent a threat to it cannot always be so categorically distinguished. There were times when it seemed that life and the attachments that made it might give way, that the possibility of living on might come undone. Solitude seemed to be a force in this undoing. But, as I describe below, it was also folded into sociality at Walter Reed.

Solitude and Biosocial Life

Solitude, as much as queer multiplicity, sometimes appears as an untenable state in social theorizations of the normative worlds of liberal modernity. In Giorgio Agamben's "bare life" or João Biehl's state of "ex-humanity," for example,[26] conditions understood to strip away social attachments are marked by radical forms of solitude, including the solitude understood to be an effect of the limits of communication and meaning imposed by bodily pain.[27] Even queer theory's antisocial thesis hinges on the multiplicity of monstrous nonmultipliers,[28] and the utopian refutation of it is clearly articulated in the collective language of *we*.[29] In these ways, critical renderings of practices of living often seem oriented toward stable social connection, and critical renderings of practices of dying seem oriented toward solitary bodies. But ways of being (rather than ways of not being) are also constituted through pain, suffering, abandonment, and death. Fleshy, ethical, political, and even symbolic social worlds emerge through practices of negotiating the possibilities of precarious life and death in community or, at least, in common with others,[30] through keeping watch with others,[31] or the ethical responsiveness of remaining.[32] And, I suggest, amid the in-durable socialities of the precarious present, solitude can be like this, too.

At Walter Reed, solitude was an inescapable but ambiguous feature of life, one that was as much a banal part of the everyday as it was a harbinger of deadly harm, and sometimes a kind of refuge from it. Many of the seemingly endless hours of empty time that soldiers faced—after a morning of appointments and in the absence of a special support-the-troops event like a trip to a baseball game or a steak dinner out—were spent in solitary distraction, watching TV or movies or playing video games in one's own room. This was a solitude held in common, a normal way of being alone and one that could sometimes be shared with others. It was part of the in-durable sociality that soldiers shared. But solitude could also become a cause of special concern, both institutionally and among soldiers and families themselves.

There was also a relatively new rule at Walter Reed that injured soldiers were not allowed to spend the night alone. One civilian employee who had been working at Walter Reed for decades explained to me that the main reason for it was to prevent suicides. He told me of one dark rumor involving a leap from the top of a multistory parking lot on post, but I never heard any others, and it seemed there had been only one documented suicide at Walter Reed in the post-9/11 era. But this explanation for why soldiers couldn't spend the night alone didn't require such deaths or their evidence to make sense. As military suicide rates surpassed both civilian suicide rates (which historically have been higher) and numbers of combat deaths, a moral panic set in, making suicide a special focus of the way that violence and death are seen to stick to US soldiers.[33] In this context, being alone, perhaps especially during the long quiet stretches of solitary nights, is seen to be such a hazard at Walter Reed that it has been forbidden. Soldiers are not allowed to sleep alone. The rule was directed at nothing more than maintaining life itself, directed at the prevention of death but not at the fortification of forms of life.

Though suicide was exceedingly rare at Walter Reed, being alone at night could still bring death close. And at the same time, and in ways such a rule could never capture, instances of being alone at night were bound up with forms of being with that sustained life in the present. The social fortifications of a life did not simply give way to a vortex of solitary death. They remained tangled up in a kind of precarious suspension. Jake, for example, was sometimes confronted with spending the night alone after his wife, Tanielle, was put on bed rest and remained back home in South Carolina. His mother had moved nearby to be close to him, and though he could spend the night at her house, he would have to get up so early in the morning to make it back for formation or appointments that he wouldn't be able to take his sleep meds, and without his sleep meds he would have horrible nightmares, in which case, like many soldiers at Walter Reed, he'd rather not sleep at all. Some nights Manny could stay with him in his room—and this was what the rule advised, to find a "Battle Buddy" to bunk with, using the army term for combat comrades designated to look out for each other, taking care to look for signs of suicidality and post-traumatic stress disorder. But it wasn't always possible, and given the way it intimated lasting homosocial intimacies that could displace the family forms future life was supposed to orient toward, it didn't seem to them like a proper solution for the present. And anyway, someone had donated special orthopedic mattresses to the Fisher House that made Jake's back ache and ruined his days, so maybe it was best to stay up all night at his mother's place after all. There were also those few weekend nights that Jake spent alone driving six hours each way back and forth to South Carolina to see Tanielle, though once he had to pull over to the side of the road to take a nap so he didn't fall asleep at the wheel. And then, after he and Tanielle split up, he moved into his own room in the barracks and spent every night alone: he was lucky enough to get one of the new wheelchair-accessible barracks rooms with a little kitchenette, but these newly built rooms meant to accommodate the bodies of severely injured soldiers were singles. Those few lucky soldiers that got them *had* to spend the night alone. For Jake, all these ways of breaking the rule, all these ways of sleeping alone, were also ways of managing social attachments, of deciding who to be with and who to be without and of becoming sensitive to what those decisions felt like, in every sense of the word. Managing the configuration of social attachments was a way of supporting or imperiling his life and his flesh: feelings of comfort, restlessness, fear, exhaustion, and pain. All of these feelings were measures of his condition in both a social and a clinical sense.

. . .

When Daniel was told his new job was "EOD" he Googled it to find out what it meant: Explosives Ordinance Disposal. When he ended up at Walter Reed, his wife and their baby joined him. His wife's sister visited often, taking care of the baby and taking a break from the chaos of her own life back in Tennessee to shore up her sister's. Daniel was not often around, though I spent lots of time with his wife, Sam. Daniel's leg had been badly damaged in an IED blast, and soon after he arrived at the Fisher House it became clear that it wasn't going to get any better. Sam would sometimes coax him out of their bedroom and onto the living room couch, where he would sit silently, sometimes scowling, sometimes smiling at their son, Little J, who looked just like him. When I spoke to him, he smiled politely and said as little as possible. Even in the company of others he often managed to be alone. He never joined us for the communal dinners we sometimes cooked. He almost always ate in his room, Sam shuffling down the hall with a plate of chicken nuggets or a grilled cheese sandwich with mayonnaise, the way she'd taught herself to make it.

Daniel's preference for solitude was talked about and treated as a cause for concern by others. Other injured soldiers tried to get him to hang out in the parking lot while they worked on their cars, to no avail. It was big news when they convinced him to go to the mall and buy a GPS, and when they got back we all tried not to make a big deal about it, afraid we'd scare him off. His aloneness went beyond what was held in common by other soldiers, past the limit of in-durability, even though he shared his room with his wife, baby, and sister-in-law. In fact, while the continued presence of these others might have seemed like a social prophylactic against suicide, his desire for solitude raised concerns about the lives of others, as it was also read as a broader sign of dangerous unpredictability. Sam and her sister Vanessa wouldn't leave the baby alone with him. If something happened to Little J, it seemed like Daniel might just let it. No matter how he tried, Daniel couldn't sever the ties that linked him to those around him. But his attempts to shake them off made those ties, the very ones sustaining the form of his life in the present, seem hazardous. They became the sites of mutual vulnerability,[34] and as he attempted to gouge out the anchors that held them fast, the diffuse concern about unpredictable, perhaps even violent, social contact proved well founded.

As we milled around in the communal dining room one night, overtaken by group of VIPs hosting a dinner at the Fisher House to show their support for injured soldiers, Vanessa told me that the night before they left Little J alone in the room with Daniel. Little J was asleep, and Daniel said he was up for it. He'd seemed a little better lately. It seemed okay. She'd gone in to check on them. As soon as she'd opened the door, Daniel jerked back, pulling a pillow away from Little J's head. Vanessa screamed at him, demanding to know what he was doing. He said he was just trying to make the baby more comfortable. Vanessa said that was bullshit: he was trying to kill him, to smother him with a pillow—it was obvious.

Vanessa was sure that if she hadn't gone to check on them, Little J would be dead. She'd taken Little J out of the room. She'd told Sam. She was furious. She didn't know what else to do. The consequences of reporting it to a military police officer or his commanding officer would probably make things worse, rather than better. But they wouldn't leave Little J alone with Daniel anymore.

Then we heard a ruckus outside, some shouting, but nothing that disrupted the casual special occasion in the dining room. It seemed to be coming from the parking lot. It was followed by a silence. A friend went out to check. A few minutes later I followed and found him standing next to Sam, who was leaning on her rented car, eyes red and still dripping with tears. Daniel had tried to leave, to get into the car and take off. Sam had tried to stop him. In his condition, with his useless leg, on his medications, and in his wild state, it was hard to imagine how he could survive any length of time behind the wheel. But she'd kept that to herself. Instead she'd reminded Daniel that soldiers aren't allowed to drive the cars rented for their families by the Yellow Ribbon Fund. He had insisted he needed to leave. She had insisted that he not drive himself anywhere. And that's when he lifted up one of his crutches and swung it at her with all his might, hitting her square on the side of the head. Then, leaving one crutch on the ground and one sticking out of the trunk, he'd taken off limping painfully into the contained darkness of Walter Reed.

During the night they found him. He hadn't even made it to the front gate. They put him on the locked psych ward for three days. On the second day, Sam reluctantly went to visit him, but only because she needed the car keys that Daniel said he would only give to her. Now that he was locked away, in an enforced solitude of someone else's design, he used the little leverage he had left to pull her to him. He tells her it's horrible in there, that he doesn't belong in there, that there are really crazy people in there, talking to themselves and worse. He also tells her that he doesn't have the keys, that he threw them into the grass that night. He doesn't seem entirely sure why. He lied about it so she would come to him, so he wouldn't feel abandoned to the imposed isolation of the ward where the people who share it with him don't even seem to live in a shared present.

Daniel is made to talk to a psychiatrist, and Sam goes with him a couple of times. Later she explains to me what his desperate need for solitude was about. He told her that ever since he'd left Iraq, he'd look into anyone's face and know they were trying to kill him. This was why he stayed in their room. This was why he never went to the mall. This was why he'd tried to smother Little J. In a kind of inversion of Levinasian ethics, where the face carries the injunction not to kill,[35] every face-to-face encounter was a moment of kill or be killed. That night he'd tried to take off in a desperate attempt to save himself, but also to save those faces he couldn't help but see, those most intimate to him. Solitude had seemed like the only possible continuation of life, the only way to avoid death, even if it meant a kind of withdrawal and solitude more extreme than what he could manage in that shared room, surrounded by some thin version of kith and kin. But faced with the decayed sociality of the psych ward, he did his best to be with others, getting Sam to come to him.

After he got out of the psych ward, things were a bit better. Though eventually he stopped going to the psychiatrists, complaining that all they wanted to talk about was Iraq, he kept taking his new meds. His need for solitude was less overwhelming, his mode of being with others less deadly, more in-durable. Though he still rarely spent time with other soldiers, it was no longer because their faces were a threat to his life. It was now, at least in part, because he felt guilty that he wasn't as badly injured as some of them were and was worried that they'd think he didn't have a right to be there; in place of a need to sever the attachments he had, there was a fear that the affiliations available to him might be untenable.

This story of Daniel, the way that death mediated his relationship to his wife and baby son, and the way that solitude was both a sign of potential death and an unsustainable refuge from it, is exceptional. It describes a rare instance in which the various nearnesses of death confront a soldier with a choice between a social death of radical solitude and a biological death of intimacy and attachment. But as an exceptional case it speaks to, and even demonstrates, habits and tacit understandings of the contours of a vital and precarious sociality. Though people at Walter Reed hardly ever do what he did, Daniel's solitude was readily legible to those around him as a sign of deadly danger. His explanation that everyone around him—even his baby boy—was trying to kill him was instantly comprehensible, even to Sam, and no one I spoke with ever called it into question. This common sense holds people together in moments when the ramifying and multiple violence of war tears them apart. It also makes solitude legible as a life-preserving practice, and as a form of life preservation that cannot sustain a future.

The Future That Does Not Come

Both now and throughout its century-long wartime history, Walter Reed has been a place doubly governed by American fantasies of the good life. As a site for the remaking of lives as well as the salvaging of limbs, it has always had the rehabilitative mission of "remaking of men" in whatever normative and socially productive (and always raced, classed, and gendered) form ruled the day.[36] And as a key publicized space of the American wartime imaginary, it has been a site for staging nationally redemptive stories of violence that hinge on the triumph and restoration of soldier bodies.

But while Walter Reed is so governed by normative fantasies of self, sociality, and time, it is also uncongenial to their achievement. It is not a place where such fantasies can actually be realized. The experience of living in it doesn't conform to the temporalities of rehabilitation that guide clinical models,[37] or to those ideal trajectories of recovery on which redemptive national narratives are based. It is a place, as Jake said, where you have to wait around. Though the site was governed as if it were a space for reassembling a salvaged future, being at Walter Reed was a practice of biding time among bits and pieces, living through in-durable socialities of a precarious present rather than forging the solid contours of a world to come.

At a broader social and cultural level, the conventionalized sociality of conjugal couplehood, and the ethical and biopolitical investments it is bound up with, also helped smooth the path to the post-9/11 wars in the first place, both through ethical investments that unevenly distribute the value of life across political geographies[38] and through social investments in fantasies of the good life all the more easily leveraged into military recruitment in an increasingly depressed, falsely nostalgic, and eternally optimistic, American dreamscape. For those soldiers whose lives are most marked by war's violence, it is not at all clear how or why such an unmarked ordinary world would be possible or even, in many ways, better than a life that made space for the fractures of war's transformations or for forms of sociality that could more thoroughly embrace them. Such a desire for soldiers to settle into an unchanged ordinary after everything has changed seems both optimistic and cruel in Berlant's sense, an investment, attachment, or "desire that is actually an obstacle to . . . flourishing."[39] What is lost in pursuit of such a narrow form of life? What would have happened, for example, if Jake hadn't gotten married at all but had opened that garage with Manny instead? What's more, though rehabilitation and reintegration are the watchwords of this optimism, return is not, in fact, the desirable outcome, given that so many soldiers join the military because of the structural instabilities of their lives—unemployment, for example, or the inaccessibility of higher education, or the absence of other life choices in the rural swaths of the country where formerly reliable industries and livelihoods have vanished. This past is not the future soldiers hope for, nor is it the one that public policy and private organizations envision. As the relentless and desperate chorus of American (anti)politics has it, tomorrow must be better and brighter than today.[40]

There remain, as always, alternatives to such fantasies, like the social critique, camaraderie, and, sometimes, informal experiments in communal living of the national organization Iraq Veterans against the War, itself modeled on the Vietnam Veterans against the War organization, which created alternative affective, social, and political spaces for veterans, all of which were part of the infrastructure of social, cultural, and political change in the Vietnam War era. But such alternatives get little traction against the overwhelming pull of normative sociality that is so culturally and institutionally supported as a bulwark against the forms of death and pathologized sociality and solitude that many soldiers seem unable to shake. Many injured soldiers do indeed find ways, as Jake could not, to pick up the pieces of a fractured world and assemble them, with some assistance, into a version of properly configured good life. But many others manage to hang on by finding in-durable sociality rather than stability amid or out of those fragments.

A study of Vietnam veterans found that the small percentage of them whose posttraumatic stress disorder diagnosis persisted through the decades after the war were twice as likely as those who no longer had the diagnosis to die prematurely, "their lives often claimed by the rough hand of a life on the margins: injuries, accidents, suicide and homicide."[41] Responding to the report, a representative of Vietnam Veterans of America was careful not to condemn the services of the VA, though in terms that suggest hanging on, merely being alive rather than dead, may be all that veterans have to show for decades of care: "We know a lot of people who are alive today because of the V.A. medical centers," he said. "They may not be getting better, but they're not offing themselves."[42] Attending ethnographically to sociality and forms of life in such protracted zones of afterwar precarity—including the temporally circumscribed one found at Walter Reed—is thus not a project that offers a hopeful picture of an emerging world. Nor is it an attention justified by the search for, or locating of, immanent critique. It is instead an attention to a significant and evanescent present, one that can convey and illuminate certain impasses of life in the contemporary American afterwar, for all that those are worth.

In their ethnographic unfolding, these scenes of solitude that may gesture toward social death or life itself are accompanied by in-durable sociality, sometimes so thin or transient or analytically awkward or seemingly unsubstantial that an analysis of social life might too easily treat it as negligible. But it is certainly not negligible in this context where aloneness is explicitly marked as dangerous and linked to the comorbid risks of social and biological death, all while being wrapped up in various forms of affiliation, attachment, and specifically calibrated measures of concern.

We can easily view in such scenes a conventional anthropological distinction between the suffering individual whose increasingly solitary body is bound to the temporality of crisis, and the redemptive possibility of a future sociality that looks more whole and more vital, more entire and more social, than the precarious and materially overdetermined present,[43] a future where life has some breathing room. On the one hand, we find precarious lives, suffering bodies, and the comorbid conditions of social and biological death and, on the other, stable and communal social forms and a redeemable and even hopeful future. But in thinking the in-durable, I have tried to focus on the present in the way it is attended to in the moments I encountered it, tracing out the qualities of sociality, intimacy, and ethical attachment that accompany or are capacitated by a multiplicity of individuated and enfleshed people in pain.

These are the qualities of a in-durable sociality, an ordinariness that adheres in a precarious present, giving it its ethical substance and then giving way to social formations that may not be qualitatively new, may not be redemptively collective, and may instead snatch normativity from the jaws of the otherwise. In-durable sociality at Walter Reed is thin and brittle and unenduring; it has no future of its own, it is not transformative, *and* it is vitally important to the sustaining of life at Walter Reed.

If we tie ethical attachment and intimacy to a more stable and recognizable social world to come, we risk displacing ethics, intimacy, care, and sociality altogether from scenes of precarious life. The ethical substance of precarious life shared in common with others is put beside the point. A collective future, even if deferred through the temporality of emergency, might hold out the possibility that worthless suffering may prove to have been otherwise. But what happens when the future comes and brings, for example, the death and forgetting of a generation, or the fizzling out of a movement that never was, or the gradual dispersal of shared intensities into the wind of liberal autological selfhood?

Precarity can seem, again, like a past property of individual lives (albeit politically situated ones). Suffering can seem like the ordeal of a solitary body (albeit a socially structured phenomenon). In-durable socialities can be diagnosed as social failures; and deathbound lives, as little more than the end points where layers of inequality finally compress and crush the body. Ethical attachments may be rendered invisible, exempted from history, or made to seem worthless, if they do not emerge as a pivotal chapter in a morally valued story, if the moment does not rise to the level of an event.

A form of sociality, like the one shared by injured soldiers, thrown into being in a social or political space of some consequence, like Walter Reed, may be consequential without being transformative. It is here that we find the way suicide becomes shared as a "way of life" across generations of dispossession, as Angela Garcia has described; what Lisa Stevenson suggests we might think of as "life beside itself," sad and uncanny experiences of affection, intimacy, and care that cross the necropolitical line between life and death; and the modes of collective endurance in a cruddy world that is historically drawn and redrawn into the brackets of white settler liberalism's fantasies that Elizabeth Povinelli has traced.[44] It is how such thoroughly and already bio- and necropolitical subjects live on among themselves, how they do something other than protest or seek to collectively constitute themselves within or against new regimes of legibility, how they "shelter in place" or bide their time or wait for nothing but the next thing to happen.[45] It matters without promising much for the future. It is a way of enduring in a difficult present that itself desires to endure.

So, if we more readily complement hopeful questions about emergence with others that put hope in abeyance, if we can divest ourselves of our special attachment to "miracles of enduring difference,"[46] we may more readily see, for example, how the sustaining of life in the present can depend on forms of care and ethical attachment and structures of biopolitical capacitation that do not transform worlds, even fragmented ones, but consequentially (and cruelly) remake them much as they have been, even in times of endemic or acute crisis or fragmentation or structured suffering that would seem ripe for transformation into an otherwise world.

Notes

1. See Naisargi N. Dave's contribution in this issue.

2. Han, "Symptoms of Another Life."

3. Kafer, *Feminist, Queer, Crip*; see also Weeks, *Problem with Work*.

4. Berlant, *Cruel Optimism*.

5. See, e.g., Hetherington and Junger, *Infidel*, 200–201; and Thorpe, *Soldier Girls*.

6. Povinelli, *Economies of Abandonment*, 13. Because the moment of afterwar life I describe here is situated within many other events, from the historical transformations of American military and security practice following 9/11 to the periodic scandals about veterans' access to health care, I find helpful Povinelli's distinction between those forms of suffering that rise to the level of an event and those that do not. But I recognize that other analytical traction might be gained from rethinking the quasi event in other ways, as Veena Das suggests in *Affliction*, 12–19.

7. Berlant, *Cruel Optimism*.

8. Foucault, *Discipline and Punish*; Foucault, "Friendship as a Way of Life."

9. Badiou, *Logic of Worlds*.

10. Locke and Biehl, "Deleuze and the Anthropology of Becoming."

11. See, e.g., Das, *Affliction*; Garcia, *Pastoral Clinic*; Povinelli, *Empire of Love*; and Povinelli, *Economies of Abandonment*.

12. These rough numbers are based on Fischer, "Casualty Statistics," and Walter Reed Army Medical Center, "Walter Reed Fact Sheet, June 2008," www.wramc.army.mil/Lists/WRNews/DispForm.aspx?ID=85 (accessed 30 September 2010).

13. The name nonmedical attendant (NMA) was somewhat erroneous, given that NMAs could be responsible for things like daily wound care and the maintenance of medication regimes, as well as the less explicitly medicalized tasks that could range from help bathing to doing paperwork. On the NMA program, see Wool and Messinger, *Labors of Love*.

14. Jain, *Malignant*; Lorde, *Cancer Journals*; Wegenstein, *Good Breast and the Bad Breast.*

15. See, e.g., Anderson, *Imagined Communities*; Canaday, *Straight State*; and Mosse, *Image of Man.*

16. Linker, *War's Waste*, 14–17; Skocpol, *Protecting Soldiers and Mothers.*

17. Linker, *War's Waste*, esp. 30–31.

18. Frydl, *G.I. Bill*, 2. The action ended in disaster when General Douglas MacArthur sent in the army, violently destroying the encampment. Dramatic and fiery scenes were captured on film and shown, to the horror of fellow Depression-suffering Americans, on newsreels and in newspapers around the country. Dickson and Allen, *Bonus Army*; Waters and White, *B.E.F.*

19. A similar, though more dystopic, sociality was seen to arise from the fetid wards of overflowing VA hospitals during the era of the Vietnam War, captured, for example, in Hal Ashby's 1978 film *Coming Home.* In that film, heterosexual couplehood strongly rooted in sexual intimacy and orgasmic satisfaction ultimately provides a release from the ward and its sociality, as well as from its forms of institutional debility and humiliation. The failure of the normative couplehood is also inextricably bound up with the failure of life, triggering the suicidal violence supposed to be embedded in veterans. In Robert Zemeckis's 1994 film *Forrest Gump* it is the love and devotion of fellow veteran Forrest Gump that saves the injured veteran Lt. Dan from a thinner, more solitary world, though ultimately the lives of both Forrest and Lt. Dan are secured and redeemed by normative forms of true, heteronormative love and marriage.

20. Egendorf, "Vietnam Veteran Rap Groups."

21. More than just the relationship we name with the terms *husband* and *wife*, conjugal couplehood is a "key transfer point within liberalism" (Povinelli, *Empire of Love*, 17) and basic social unit of normative American life through which discourses and practices of normative selfhood and enfleshment migrate, reside, and calibrate acceptable and pathological persons and socialities.

22. Cited in Lambek, *Weight of the Past*, x.

23. While prevalent forms of homonormativity suggest that the repeal of Don't Ask, Don't Tell may not trouble this ideal, the growing numbers of injured female veterans may trouble it, given how they may challenge the gendered arrangements of care that heteronormative couplehood entails. Only a small handful of women were at Walter Reed during my time there, but Jennifer Terry in "Significant Injury" has raised important questions about the way the biopolitics of America's post-9/11 wars intersects with national imaginaries of women's bodies in the case of war injury.

24. Wool, *After War.*

25. Wool, *Attachments of Life.*

26. Agamben, *Homo Sacer*; Biehl, *Vita*, 317–18.

27. Scarry, *Body in Pain.*

28. Edelman, *No Future.*

29. Muñoz, *Cruising Utopia.*

30. Lingis, *Community*; Livingston, *Improvising Medicine*, 120–21; Petryna, *Life Exposed*; Povinelli, *Empire of Love*; Povinelli, *Economies of Abandonment*; Taylor, "On Recognition."

31. Garcia, *Pastoral Clinic.*

32. Stevenson, *Life beside Itself.*

33. See MacLeish, "Suicide and the Governance of Military Life."

34. Butler, *Precarious Life*, 27–32.

35. Levinas, *Totality and Infinity.*

36. Linker, *War's Waste.*

37. Messinger, "Rehabilitation Time."

38. See Butler, *Frames of War*; Butler, *Precarious Life*; Povinelli, *Empire of Love*; and Povinelli, *Economies of Abandonment.*

39. Berlant, *Cruel Optimism*, 1.

40. See Edelman, *No Future.*

41. Carey, *Combat Stress.* Those who maintained the diagnosis were those whose symptoms continually met the diagnostic criteria *and* who remained in contact with the mental health professionals who wield it.

42. Ibid.

43. See, e.g., Farmer, "On Suffering"; Nordstrom, *Different Kind of War Story*; and Scheper-Hughes, "Talent for Life."

44. Garcia, *Pastoral Clinic*, 94; Povinelli, *Economies of Abandonment*; Stevenson, *Life beside Itself.*

45. On biding time and related modes of inhabiting daily life, especially in the place of devastation, see Das, *Life and Words.*

46. Povinelli, *Economies of Abandonment*, xi.

References

Agamben, Giorgio. 1998. *Homo Sacer: Sovereign Power and Bare Life.* Stanford, CA: Stanford University Press.

Anderson, Benedict. 2006. *Imagined Communities: Reflections on the Origin and Spread of Nationalism.* London: Verso.

Badiou, Alain. 2009. *The Logic of Worlds: Being and Event.* Vol. 2. Translated by Alberto Toscano. New York: Continuum.

Berlant, Lauren. 2011. *Cruel Optimism.* Durham, NC: Duke University Press.

Biehl, João. 2005. *Vita: Life in a Zone of Social Abandonment.* Berkeley: University of California Press.

Butler, Judith. 2004. *Precarious Life: The Power of Mourning and Violence.* London: Verso.

Butler, Judith. 2009. *Frames of War: When Is Life Grievable?* London: Verso.

Canaday, Margot. 2009. *The Straight State: Sexuality and Citizenship in Twentieth-Century America.* Princeton, NJ: Princeton University Press.

Carey, Benedict. 2014. "Combat Stress among Veterans Is Found to Persist since Vietnam." *New York Times*, 7 August. www.nytimes.com/2014/08/08/us/combat-stress-found-to-persist-since-vietnam.html.

Das, Veena. 2007. *Life and Words.* Berkeley: University of California Press.

Das, Veena. 2015. *Affliction: Health, Disease, Poverty.* New York: Fordham University Press.

Dickson, Paul, and Thomas B. Allen. 2006. *The Bonus Army: An American Epic.* New York: Walker.

Edelman, Lee. 2004. *No Future: Queer Theory and the Death Drive.* Durham, NC: Duke University Press.

Egendorf, Arthur. 1975. "Vietnam Veteran Rap Groups and Themes of Postwar Life." *Journal of Social Issues* 31, no. 4: 111–24. dx.doi.org/10.1111/j.1540-4560.1975.tb01015.x.

Farmer, Paul. 1997. "On Suffering and Structural Violence: A View from Below." In *Social Suffering*, edited by Arthur Kleinman, Veena Das, and Margaret M. Lock, 261–83. Berkeley: University of California Press.

Fischer, Hanna. 2010. "United States Military Casualty Statistics: Operation Iraqi Freedom and Operation Enduring Freedom." RS22452. Washington, DC: Congressional Research Service.

Foucault, Michel. 1979. *Discipline and Punish: The Birth of the Prison*. New York: Vintage Books.

Foucault, Michel. 1981. "Friendship as a Way of Life." In *Ethics, Subjectivity and Truth*, edited by Paul Rabinow, 135–40. New York: New Press.

Frydl, Kathleen J. 2009. *The G.I. Bill*. Cambridge: Cambridge University Press.

Garcia, Angela. 2010. *The Pastoral Clinic: Addiction and Dispossession along the Rio Grande*. Berkeley: University of California Press.

Han, Clara. 2011. "Symptoms of Another Life: Time, Possibility, and Domestic Relations in Chile's Credit Economy." *Cultural Anthropology* 26, no. 1: 7–32. doi.org/10.1111/j.1548-1360.2010.01078.x.

Hetherington, Tim, and Sebastian Junger. 2010. *Infidel*. New York: Chris Boot.

Jain, Sarah S. Lochlann. 2013. *Malignant: How Cancer Becomes Us*. Berkeley: University of California Press.

Kafer, Alison. 2013. *Feminist, Queer, Crip*. Bloomington: Indiana University Press.

Lambek, Michael. 2002. *The Weight of the Past: Living with History in Mahajanga, Madagascar*. New York: Palgrave Macmillan.

Levinas, Emmanuel. 1980. *Totality and Infinity: An Essay on Exteriority*. New York: Springer.

Lingis, Alphonso. 1994. *The Community of Those Who Have Nothing in Common*. Bloomington: Indiana University Press.

Linker, Beth. 2011. *War's Waste: Rehabilitation in World War I America*. Chicago: University of Chicago Press.

Livingston, Julie. 2012. *Improvising Medicine: An African Oncology Ward in an Emerging Cancer Epidemic*. Durham, NC: Duke University Press.

Locke, Peter, and João Biehl. 2010. "Deleuze and the Anthropology of Becoming." *Current Anthropology* 51, no. 3: 317–51. dx.doi.org/10.1086/651466.

Lorde, Audre. 1997. *The Cancer Journals*. San Francisco: Aunt Lute Books.

MacLeish, Kenneth. 2014. "Suicide and the Governance of Military Life." Unpublished manuscript.

Messinger, Seth D. 2010. "Rehabilitating Time: Multiple Temporalities among Military Clinicians and Patients." *Medical Anthropology* 29, no. 2: 150–69. dx.doi.org/10.1080/01459741003715383.

Mosse, George L. 1998. *The Image of Man: The Creation of Modern Masculinity*. Oxford: Oxford University Press.

Muñoz, José Esteban. 2009. *Cruising Utopia: The Then and There of Queer Futurity*. New York: New York University Press.

Nordstrom, Carolyn. 1997. *A Different Kind of War Story*. Philadelphia: University of Pennsylvania Press.

Petryna, Adriana. 2002. *Life Exposed: Biological Citizens after Chernobyl*. Princeton, NJ: Princeton University Press.

Povinelli, Elizabeth. 2006. *The Empire of Love*. Durham, NC: Duke University Press.

Povinelli, Elizabeth. 2011. *Economies of Abandonment: Social Belonging and Endurance in Late Liberalism*. Durham, NC: Duke University Press.

Scarry, Elaine. 1987. *The Body in Pain*. Oxford: Oxford University Press.

Scheper-Hughes, Nancy. 2008. "A Talent for Life: Reflections on Human Vulnerability and Resilience." *Ethnos: Journal of Anthropology* 73, no. 1: 25. dx.doi.org/10.1080/00141840801927525.

Skocpol, Theda. 1995. *Protecting Soldiers and Mothers: The Political Origins of Social Policy in United States*. Cambridge, MA: Belknap Press.

Stevenson, Lisa. 2014. *Life beside Itself: Imagining Care in the Canadian Arctic*. Berkeley: University of California Press.

Taylor, Janelle S. 2008. "On Recognition, Caring, and Dementia." *Medical Anthropology Quarterly* 22, no. 4: 313–35. dx.doi.org/10.1111/j.1548-1387.2008.00036.x.

Terry, Jennifer. 2009. "Significant Injury: War, Medicine, and Empire in Claudia's Case." *Women's Studies Quarterly* 37, nos. 1/2: 200–225. dx.doi.org/10.2307/27655146.

Thorpe, Helen. 2014. *Soldier Girls: The Battles of Three Women at Home and at War*. New York: Scribner.

Waters, W. W., and William Carter White. 1933. *B.E.F.: The Whole Story of the Bonus Army*. New York: John Day.

Weeks, Kathi. 2011. *The Problem with Work: Feminism, Marxism, Antiwork Politics, and Postwork Imaginaries*. Durham, NC: Duke University Press.

Wegenstein, Bernadette. 2016. "The Good Breast and the Bad Breast: Cosmetic Surgery and Breast Cancer." In *Living and Dying in the Contemporary World: A Compendium*, edited by Veena Das and Clara Han, 382–98. Oakland: University of California Press.

Wool, Zoë H. 2015. "Attachments of Life: Intimacy, Genital Injury, and the Flesh of US Soldier Bodies." In *The Anthropology of Living and Dying in the Contemporary World*, edited by Veena Das and Clara Han, 399–417. Berkeley: University of California Press.

Wool, Zoë H. 2015. *After War: The Weight of Life at Walter Reed*. Durham, NC: Duke University Press.

Wool, Zoë H., and Seth Messinger. 2012. "Labors of Love: The Transformation of Care in the Non-medical Attendant Program at Walter Reed Army Medical Center." *Medical Anthropology Quarterly* 26, no. 1: 26–48.

The Rainy Season

Toward a Cinematic Ethnography of Crisis and Endurance in Mexico City

Angela Garcia

Carlos Reygadas's film *Post Tenebras Lux* (2012) opens with an overextended sequence of a young girl wandering through a muddy field. Shot from the perspective of the child, our attention is initially drawn to her nervous delight as cows and herding dogs crowd around her. As the camera slowly shifts to a wider view, capturing a storm gathering in the horizon, we hear the diffuse buzzing of crickets. In a close-up of the child's flushed face, we observe her rub her eyes and wet nose, the condensation of her exhaled breath. She searches the darkening field, murmuring *mami, casa, papi*, but no adult comes for her. The camera's beveled lens, which blurs the edges and sometimes center of the shot, and the film's oversaturated colors reinforce the scene's ambiguity and sensuality. Before we are able to adjust to the film's sensory mode of address or to formulate some kind of explanation for it, the screen goes black. The transitory blockage of visual and auditory fields is followed by bursts of lightning and the film's title, which appears as disconnected words.

Post Tenebras Lux, Latin for "after darkness light," is what Vivian Sobchack calls a "difficult film," a category that refers to works audiences tend to regard as hard to explain, boring, disgusting, or some combination thereof.[1] Difficult films don't "make sense" in the way we expect sense to mean—coherent, plausible, and referential—and this, Sobchack says, tends to arouse discomfort in the viewer. Several descriptions of *Post Tenebras Lux* in the popular press characterize such responses: "Lacking focus . . . it's an opaque, unforthcoming, exasperating work at the same time."[2] "Impressionistic and tantalizing . . . Viewers can expect to be plunged into obscurity rather than enlightened."[3] As one review put it, *Post Tenebras*

Social Text 130 · Vol. 35, No. 1 · March 2017
DOI 10.1215/01642472-3728020 © 2017 Duke University Press

Lux is "a patience tester [and] a waste of time . . . [that might] have paid off had it built towards some kind of satisfying emotional or intellectual finale."[4] With notable exceptions, the film's "difficulty" corresponds to negative, even hostile, descriptions of viewing it and, by extension, the conclusion that it lacks sense and meaning.

Sobchack advocates for a phenomenological model of cinematic sense premised on the spectator's intense and focused engagement with the film's specificity and, reciprocally, the sensorial experiences this engagement ignites in the spectator. Implied in this proposition is the willingness to remain open to the film's provocations or, as Sobchack puts it, to remain "focused on—rather than through" the difficult image.[5] Her formulation is suggestive for reflecting on the possibilities and tasks that exist in what is perceived as hard, meaningless, or painful and how ethnography might better view and express the "difficulty of reality" that we often encounter in our work.[6]

Post Tenebras Lux is an example of this potential in cinema, and it offers anthropology a reflexive stance on how filmic difficulty can nuance ethnographic engagements with disoriented and disorienting worlds. In this article, I draw on the film as an aesthetic and analytic guide for presenting my own research in Mexico. In broad terms, this research relates to the ever-receding fantasy of prosperity and safety for Mexico City's middle class and the texture and temporality of endurance for its vast underclass, themes that are also major concerns in Reygadas's oeuvre.[7] The ethnographic focus of this article is one of Mexico City's ubiquitous *anexos* (annexes), which names unregulated institutions of addiction treatment for people displaced by contemporary capitalism and criminal violence. *Post Tenebras Lux* references anexos in a resonant scene, which I describe later in this article. More important, the film as a whole sensorally captures something of the difficult reality anexos embody and seek to address and, precisely in so doing, helps to unseat the way anexos are conventionally understood.

Every week the Mexican media tells stories of "slaves" (*esclavos*) being rescued from the hell anexos are made to represent. They are described as filthy and dark, teeming with people "deprived of their liberty" and subjected to horrific violence.[8] Indeed, anexos' harsh living quarters and treatments do violate the narrow logics and practices that define normative frameworks of drug "recovery."[9] In this way, anexos manifest some of the same coordinates of Sobchack's difficult films: they don't make sense, as long as we assume a false dividing line between the worlds of reason and feeling. Conversely, considering the profound distaste anexos provoke on the part of their critics, and the powerful disruption they aim to induce in their patients, anexos make too much sense. The question that interests me here is the manner in which anexos produce these heightened sensorial responses, the underlying social and political stances these responses imply, and how they might inform more conscious analysis.

In putting *Post Tenebras Lux* in dialogue with my ethnography of anexos, my aim is to reflect on the interplay of difficulty and sense making and to visualize in writing the anexo as a space evoking the conditions and rhythms of crisis in Mexico, while also capacitating a will to endure it.[10] Part of this work involves reflecting on how I have come to make sense of anexos, a process facilitated by years of ethnographic fieldwork in and around them and diverse scholarly engagements focused on precarious socialities.[11] Just as influential are experiences of critically reflecting on films that make visible and affecting the historical and structural conditions that result in specific embodied experiences and social formations in Mexico today. Reygadas's *Post Tenebras Lux* is exemplary in this regard, as its aesthetic apprehension of these conditions defamiliarizes the too familiar images and narratives of poverty and violence in Mexico.[12] Instead, it slowly awakens the viewer's senses to the interior struggles of its characters that arise out of specific material and political realities. The film's fabulation of these realities begins with what is *felt* as difficulty: ambivalence, boredom, confusion, exhaustion, pain, subordination, vulnerability, and unevenness—in short, sensory and perceptual modes that manifest the existential contingency presented in the film.[13] These felt expressions demand the viewer's attention and interaction, which may foster new forms of sensory experience and analysis.

At this juncture, it would be helpful to briefly describe the story *Post Tenebras Lux* tells. It focuses on a privileged couple from Mexico City raising two young children in Mexico's countryside. Juan is an architect and is estranged from his beautiful wife, Natalia. Much of the film is shot in and around their house, which is actually Reygadas's house, as are the two children that appear in the film. Juan and Natalia's estate (that is, Reygadas's) is a vision of rural life articulated from an affluent, urban perspective: it's modern, bright, and open to edenic surroundings. The couple seems to get along with the locals, whom they depend on for labor, but profound class and ethnic differences stand between them. A palpable tension slowly builds, revealed primarily through Juan's uneasy friendship with his handyman Siete (Seven), a recovering addict who lives in rural poverty. The story unfolds episodically, its narrative momentum slowed by prolonged long shots, extreme close-ups, and inexplicable dreamscapes. These techniques insist that the viewer is always conscious of the story being constructed and strip the events on-screen of self-evident qualities.

Like all of Reygadas's features, *Post Tenebras Lux* is shot on location and uses nonprofessional actors, who often appear awkward and conscious of the camera. Their acting skills, or lack of them, become central to the unfolding of the story and help to create awareness of the underlying relations of the film. Dialogue is sparse and often unscripted, suggesting that language alone is not an adequate means of knowing the characters. Instead, the characters, who often appear frozen into a tableau vivant, are among the images that figure in Reygadas's aesthetic project, one focused on mobilizing a sensory awareness of the underlying historicity of specific material and social realities.

For this and other reasons that will become clear shortly, *Post Tenebras Lux* offers a compelling framework for reflecting on the relationship between anexos' existential and material dimensions on the level of image and sensation rather than mere explanation. Rather than force a direct comparison between the film and anexos along these lines, I'm interested in how the film provides a logic of sense from which to construct and apprehend the difficult reality anexos embody.[14] This interest has to do not only with seeking new methodologies and resources suitable for studying anexos but also with advocating for an expanded concept of ethnography that, following contemporary film studies, "emphasizes the relevance of intertwined sensations, and the interpretation of these sensations, for the aesthetic experience of the medium."[15] Borrowing Jacques Rancière's definition of medium as also meaning "a milieu or a sensorium,"[16] this article attends to the configuration of senses and modes of perception within the mediums of the film and the anexo and probes the ramifications of how they engage with the world.

A Shelter in the Woods

A key scene in *Post Tenebras Lux* reinforces Reygadas's aesthetic sensibility and is a fitting introduction to anexos. It depicts an Alcoholics Anonymous (AA) meeting held in a remote shack in the mountains. The rural landscape is not depicted idealistically, nor is it imbued with ambiguity or melancholy, as in the opening sequence. Instead, it is depicted naturalistically, revealing it to be an impoverished, working landscape, subjected to the harsh material realities of the surrounding environment.

These realities are further epitomized by the shack itself. Lacking electricity, the building is dark and moist—the opposite of Juan's (that is, Reygadas's) modernist home. Narrow strips of light stream through the building's cracks, highlighting the skin of an old man standing behind a rustic wood podium, where he prepares to give his AA testimony. The camera lingers on a close-up of the man's deeply wrinkled skin, drawing a connection between the texture of his flesh and his environment. It then slowly pans out to show the contours of the faces that surround him. Indigenous and poor, they appear visibly uncomfortable, as if Reygadas stumbled upon the meeting while taking a walk in the woods. By consciously presenting the members' discomfort, the scene makes visible the forms of submission and subjectivization among Mexico's disenfranchised populations.

The old man behind the podium has a whispery voice. After a few vague sentences about his life, he puts on his hat and walks slowly outside the frame. Another man, restless but weary, approaches the podium. Hands behind his back, he looks directly into the camera and recounts his labor skills: electrical work, construction, and logging. He then looks away from the camera and, between deep breaths, lists his troubles with alcohol, drugs, and sex workers. He gives thanks to the fellowship, asks for strength to continue to live, and walks off.

The third man to approach the podium is Siete, Juan's handyman. Siete also begins his testimony by listing his labor skills, reinforcing its centrality for Mexico's poor. He announces the unexpected presence of his friend Juan and then quickly notes that Juan is also his boss, whom he nevertheless considers a friend. It's an awkward moment, as if Siete has been caught trying to take something that didn't belong to him, foreshadowing events to come. The camera shifts from Siete to Juan, who sits apart from the members, close to the door. Juan is flooded in natural light, making his light skin appear even lighter.

When the AA meeting ends, Juan and Siete move outside. Siete dusts off a chair for Juan, who sits, and then leans against the shack's wall, which is composed of banged-together materials. The sounds of clucking chickens and chainsaws reverberate in the distance. After a long stretch of silence, Siete speaks to Juan about his childhood. He tells him about his alcoholic parents, getting high at the age of thirteen, situations of domestic violence, his life growing increasingly out of control, and his eventual "internment" in an anexo, where he finally got clean. But after spending seven months in the anexo (thus, presumably, his name "Seven"), Siete returned home to find that his wife and children had left him. His hoped-for future, which hinged on his recovery in an anexo, did not materialize.

Recovery is a concept central to addiction and the neoliberal Mexican state. In both contexts, the concept embraces the individualization of health, wealth, and the potentiality of being, either through a process of personal transcendence or by social and economic reform. In this scene, recovery loses any self-evident meaning or pretension to actuality. Instead, it refers to a mode of life whose major theme is the common work of endurance. This is expressed visually by the meeting in a shack, a figuration of sociality in late liberal "economies of abandonment," to use Elizabeth Povinelli's term.[17] The battered shack is a space of affiliation for individuals trying to maintain their footing in terms of not only their sobriety but also the harsh conditions in which they live.

Siete falls silent, and the camera rests on his downward-looking face, apprehending his exhaustion. Eventually, it cuts to Juan seated against a backdrop of a desolate-looking forest, a visual negation of his fantasy of rural enchantment. Siete asks Juan what his problem is. Juan hesitatingly responds that he doesn't really have a problem, just issues with Internet pornography, which leave him unable to have sex with his wife. Juan stands, casually touches Siete's arm, and tells him, "Let's go."

This sequence conjures up the huge gap between Mexico's privileged and the poor, a gap that rests, in part, upon the state forsaking its historic role as defender of the poor. The Mexican Revolution in 1910 was fought in reaction to long-standing liberal policies that concentrated land and wealth among a tiny elite class, leaving the rest of the country in abject poverty. The resulting Mexican Constitution sought to reverse this through widespread social reforms. However, after more than two decades of neoliberal recovery, Mexico has shifted back to remarkably severe labor precarization and has witnessed continuous deterioration of the majority of the population's living conditions.[18] The image of the shack, the frequent references to informal labor in the AA testimonies, and Siete's history in an anexo imply this history. Siete is in "crisis"; Juan is not. This is not to say that Juan is without struggle; his admission conveys a degree of alienation. The point is that Siete's and Juan's struggles with poverty and excess, abandonment and disillusionment, are analogous to the differential conditions of life under late capitalism.

This brief AA scene marks the first time I encountered a perspective on anexos that did not condemn them as criminal or unethical. On the contrary, the scene is striking for its simplicity, for the solemnity of its mood, and for the critical presence of Juan. Although the anexo Siete recalls is not cinematically represented, it is powerfully evoked. Mediated through the contemporaneous perspectives of the two protagonists, the anexo, like the shack, is a lens from which to consider the extreme imbalances that characterize contemporary Mexican life.

Testimony

Anexos were conceived in Mexico City in the mid-1970s with the establishment of Mexico's twenty-four-hour "intensive" AA groups. Departing from traditional AA and its insistence on voluntary membership and ninety-minute meetings, Mexico's twenty-four-hour groups offered meetings around the clock and embraced a confrontational, Roman Catholic sensibility. They also offered anexos where homeless or chronically ill alcoholics could live while sobering up. The anexo was therefore originally designed as a shelter and meeting place for poor alcoholics attending a culturally adapted form of AA. Today, they are the most accessible and widely used form of residential treatment for drug addiction in Mexico.

Although there is no formal history on anexos, my research suggests they evolved within the context of Mexico's many "crises"—financial debt, austerity, and the so-called drug war—that have beset the country for decades.[19] Serenity, the anexo that I focus on here, emerged within the tensions of these crises. It was established in 1995, the same year the peso lost 50 percent of its value against the US dollar, and a year after the North American Free Trade Agreement (NAFTA) went into effect. This context of economic crisis and neoliberalization affected the residents of Iztapalapa, the Mexico City borough in which Serenity is located, in profound and lasting ways, including mass job displacement, rising unemployment, wage reductions, and the privatization of basic public services and health care.

Serenity's founder is Padrino Alfonso—*padrino* being the name given to founders and leaders of anexos. A construction worker by trade, Padrino Alfonso helped build many of the pedestrian bridges that crossed Mexico City's busy highways. It was dangerous work and resulted in serious physical injuries for him, including partial paralysis. By his forties, Padrino Alfonso was "too broken and old" to compete in a sector saturated with younger workers, and at a time when construction projects had slowed dramatically. He established Serenity to address the problem of alcoholism and despair among his peers.

Serenity opened its doors on 3 May, the Day of the Holy Cross, the feast day for construction workers. At the time it housed five residents, or *anexados*. In 2005 there were no fewer than fifteen anexados, many in their mid-twenties and addicted to crack cocaine, not alcohol. The shift registered the changing situations of addiction at a particular historical conjuncture: it was one decade after NAFTA and one year before the drug war would officially commence in Mexico.

It is unknown how many anexos exist, but public health officials estimate that there are around seventy thousand throughout the country and four thousand in Mexico City. (By contrast, there are only sixty-five "regulated" residential addiction rehabilitation centers in Mexico City, a megalopolis of over twenty-one million people.) Most anexos are run and utilized by the "informal" working poor, who comprise more than half of Mexico's population. Anexos are concentrated in areas that lack basic public infrastructure, schools, health care facilities, legal protection, and legal-sector jobs. These are areas that have also experienced an intensification of violence related to the drug war. Their inhabitants thus carry the burden of their own care, protection, and survival. Anexos embody and render this burden, both in their harsh material conditions and in their therapeutic practices.

Most anexados are committed involuntarily and arrive via a form of ritualized kidnapping that reproduces and magnifies the criminal violence that they are exposed to in daily life. Their families pay for this service, as well as a monthly fee for their relative's treatment.[20] Anexados remain confined until they are claimed by relatives, their relatives are unable to pay, or they are able to escape. Rarely are they deemed successfully rehabilitated.

For many residents of anexos I spoke to, being anexado means being "stuck." It means having to sleep, eat, exercise, cook, clean, pray, confess, and be physically and psychologically "disciplined" in the same space at the same time, day after day. This restricted milieu reflects the experiential dimensions of crisis and endurance in Mexico. Take testimony, which fills most of the day in anexos. During this practice, one by one anexados stand behind a wood podium facing their peers. At the counselors' command, the anexados are pressed to sink and dwell, in both content and form, in the misery of their lives, which is also the misery of their time. Such work often involves a return to scenes from brutal childhoods and relationships, accounts of violence and exploitative labor, or memories of murdered and disappeared relatives. One testimony may last for several hours and is usually accompanied by yelling, cigarette smoking, and intermittent stretches of silence and weeping. Meanwhile, the rest of the anexados are forced to sit still, watch, and listen, becoming in a sense the very embodiment of endurance.

Consider the testimonies of Neto, which usually revolved around El Hoyo (the Hole), the makeshift neighborhood where Neto was born and lived most of his twenty-two years. Located near an abandoned mine, El Hoyo is a settlement built on one of the precarious hillsides that frame Mexico City. Its official name is La Joya (the Jewel), a designation that conceals the violent exclusions through which the neighborhood was constituted. Most of the self-built homes are one or two rooms in size, many with earthen floors and with rooftops made of recycled materials. Water is scarce, electricity is stolen, and formal employment and public services are nonexistent; drugs, on the other hand, are widespread. The reconfiguration of La Joya as El Hoyo by its inhabitants is more than an ironic gesture—it disrupts the fantasy of inclusion and shared prosperity, realigning the neighborhood's name with its actual material and existential conditions.

One summer afternoon in 2012, Neto's testimony was animated once again by the *el derrumbe* (the landslide), which had become a motif in his testimonies. Landslides and flooding are common events for those living in informal neighborhoods along Mexico City's periphery, especially in the summer, and Neto survived more than one. During his testimonies, however, he tended to speak of them as one ongoing disaster. "It made a sound. *Whoooooosh*. It sounds like that. *Whooosh*." After registering the noise multiple times, Neto recalled the wreckage that followed the hillside's collapse, beginning with his own body. "There was shit in my eyes, ears, mouth, up to my knees. Thick . . . I'm walking, nowhere to go . . . stepping on things I can't see." Neto stepped in front of the podium and used his body to construct images. When he spoke, he shifted tenses and moved from the first to the second person, as if to enfold his audience.

> The shit sucked my pants off. You're walking with no pants on. Your dick disappeared. You see dogs digging themselves out of the mud. There's gonna be lots for them to eat but nothing for you. . . .
>
> Everything is covered in grime . . . onions, plastic bottles, broken chairs. I think I see my mother. You see her?
>
> Sister was with grandmother that day, higher up the hill. I go up, mother goes down. I don't want to look. . . .
>
> What do you find? People digging, making piles. *Help me, you motherfucker! Help me, you worthless piece of shit!* Sister is on grandmother's back. She is holding a spoon.

The singularities of Neto's testimony, which lasted for over two hours, and those in *Post Tenebras Lux*'s AA scene are striking. I cannot do justice to them here other than to note what they broadly reveal and make possible. Within the dislocation of the anexo's space-time, testimony is the anexado's fabulation of living. Neto's testimony is exemplary in this regard, as his aesthetic rendering of the landslide makes El Hoyo come alive for his audience, so that they can perceive its lethality via the interplay of moving images and sensation. In the film, the speakers' testimonies convey only the most basic plot points about their lives. But coupled with the camera's extreme close-ups of faces and still shots that emphasize the material reality of their surroundings, these fragments take on a tactile quality. In this sense, the scenes presented in Neto's testimony and in the film resonate with what Laura Marks theorizes as "haptic visuality," a mode of address that enables the audience to contemplate a sensorial vision of the human condition.[21]

The Walking Vendor

When I first began studying Serenity in 2010, it still occupied its original location in a working-class neighborhood with paved streets and food stands. The exterior of the building boasted a large banner that read "Rehabilitation Center for Alcoholics and Drug Addicts." To reach the anexo, one needed to pass through a locked metal gate that opened up onto a neat courtyard shared by two stories of apartments. Serenity was located in a corner unit on the second floor. Like the other units, it consisted of one main room approximately three hundred square feet in size, a closet-like space large enough to serve as a makeshift kitchen and office, and a water closet. Back then it housed eighteen anexados—mostly young men and women addicted to drugs from the neighborhood, sometimes even from the same building. They usually stayed three to six months, although a couple of anexados reported that they had lived there for years. Two counselors who were once anexados also lived at Serenity and assisted the padrino in its operation. Only the padrino, the counselors, and I were allowed to leave the anexo; anexados with longer periods of recovery were sometimes permitted to spend supervised time in the gated courtyard.

Padrino Francisco took over as Serenity's leader after the death of its founder, Padrino Alfonso. Neighbors in the building affectionately called Padrino Francisco *Jefe* (Boss) and often came to him with their troubles. He was, in many ways, a neighborhood success story, and he earned his good standing in the community through his ties to Serenity, where he was once anexado himself.

Like other padrinos I came to know, Padrino Francisco had little formal education. He left school at the age of eleven to help support his mother and two younger brothers, working as one of Mexico City's ubiquitous walking street vendors (*ambulantes*). He sold popsicles, fruit, cleaning supplies, and water—whatever happened to be in excess or demand. He worked six days a week, ten hours a day, his feet and throat in a perpetual state of soreness. He gave his mother the money he earned, but it was never enough. He recalled having to wear his father's shoes, which were ragged and too big. "What I hated most," he said, "was they reminded me of that motherfucker. " Padrino Francisco's father left the family when he was a young boy. "I'd rather go barefoot than wear my old man's shoes," he said. But his mother worried that he looked like a "little Indian" without them, making the family appear worse off than they really were, which was already bad enough.

That was during the 1980s, a period of economic collapse and political transition for Mexico and the growth of the drug economy. In the countryside, production of marijuana and poppy provided a better living, sometimes the only living, for a rural workforce excluded from legal jobs.[22] In urban areas, street vendors were pushed into low-level trafficking of drugs. Indeed, as a walking street vendor, Padrino Francisco added marijuana and cocaine to his list of goods. Selling drugs did not lift him out of poverty, but he was finally able to save a little money for himself. His first purchase was a pair of new black leather shoes. The day of his purchase, Francisco walked into a bar and ordered a beer. "El mundo estaba en mis manos" (The world was in my hands), he said. He was thirteen years old.

Padrino Francisco made a point of not talking with anexados about their drug-dealing activities, and I followed his lead. I came to understand such discretion as a necessary element of self-preservation. But his lack of interest in the drug histories of his anexados also expressed an essential truth: the flow of drugs was so thoroughly integrated into daily life, and had been for decades, that it was largely unremarkable. What was remarkable, however, was the spectacular violence that surrounded the drug trade, which was unleashed after former Mexican president Felipe Calderón, backed by the United States, declared "war" on drug traffickers. That occurred in December 2006, the same year Padrino Alfonso died. Since then, least 120,000 Mexicans have been killed in the drug war; another 26,000 have been disappeared, and over 250,000 Mexicans have been displaced, making it the most severe case of enforced disappearance in Latin America.[23] Padrino Francisco described Padrino Alfonso as a good man, always making and fixing things. "He timed his death well," he said, "porque no hay un manera de arreglar esta situación jodida" (because there is no way to fix this fucked-up situation).

Impasse

About halfway through *Post Tenebras Lux*, Juan and his family leave their home for a vacation. We're offered a series of shots taken from their truck in movement down a precarious rural highway. The camera shifts into an extreme close-up of the estranged couple's hands touching, as if their hands disclose the fraying narrative of a happy marriage. Natalia realizes she has left behind personal belongings that she needs for the trip. Juan dutifully turns the truck around to retrieve them. Along the way, Natalia worries *cholos* (criminals) might have already taken her things, transforming the modern airiness of their home into a place vulnerable to intruders.[24] Sharing this concern, Juan drops Natalia and their children off at an isolated roadside food stand, leaving them in the care of subordinate locals.

The scene in the ramshackle restaurant offers another opportunity to register the stark social inequalities that exist in Mexico. These inequalities are discernable in the actors' bodies: Natalia and the children are light skinned and thin; the locals have dark skin and are obese. Like the contrasting geographical milieus Reygadas establishes, the actors' bodies reveal very different realities. As Tiago de Luca puts it, "Reygadas is a topographical filmmaker, for what we have here are geographies of the earth and geographies of the flesh, and the crossroads at which these geographies overlap."[25] In this scene, the actors' bodies foreground the large-scale problem of obesity in Mexico, which stems from widespread poverty and dramatic changes to the county's diet as a consequence of NAFTA.[26]

Back home, Juan discovers Siete and an accomplice sneaking out of his property with stolen computer equipment. A brief confrontation follows. Juan asks, "What the fuck?" but Siete and his partner don't explain their actions. The camera lingers on the three men arranged in a motionless tableau. Suddenly, Juan tries to escape by running up to an outdoor patio that offers an idyllic view of the countryside. The camera tails Siete as he follows Juan and a gunshot is heard. The camera does not follow the shooting, only its understated aftermath. Toning down the violence in the scene so as to underscore its symbolic aspect, Reygadas undermines stereotypes of criminality that dominates representations of violence in contemporary Mexico. This makes room for the viewer to contemplate the conditions that produce crime and fear and to question the prevailing assumptions of blame and danger that accompany them. With this scene in mind, I return to Mexico City.

Since the start of the drug war, there was a sense that living in Mexico City was like "living in a bubble," at least for the middle and upper classes. This feeling of ease and invulnerability to the violence that had spread through the rest of the country was orchestrated though surveillance cameras, police patrols, and the gentrification of neighborhoods with financial potential. The securitization and "upgrading" of these areas occurred as far larger portions of the city fell into deeper poverty and infrastructural decay.[27] But in the summer of 2011 a palpable sense of insecurity was spreading throughout the capital. Masked criminals with weapons visited nightclubs and restaurants in the gentrified neighborhoods of Condesa, Colonia Roma, and Zona Rosa. Nurtured by a couple of high-profile cases, the threat of kidnapping preoccupied Mexico City's middle and upper classes. Most of these crimes were "express kidnappings" (*secuestro express*), in which an individual is abducted and briefly held in a "safe house" while they and their family members are drained of money. Usually, victims are physically unharmed and released within twenty-four hours.

The mainstream media speculated that "youth gangs" from Mexico City's impoverished peripheral areas were responsible for these crimes. In fact, studies have consistently shown that, since 1997, kidnappings of all types in Mexico City are far more likely to occur in poor and working-class neighborhoods.[28] Like their wealthier counterparts, vulnerable residents of these areas also employ measures to protect themselves, such as participating in armed neighborhood patrols and even placing relatives in anexos. However, according to prevailing norms of legality, such methods are largely indistinguishable from the crimes they seek to deter.

Anexos also engage in kidnappings, but in a way that cannot accurately be defined as merely "criminal." Families that arrange to have relatives kidnapped and taken to an anexo often described it as a life-extending gesture, *a prevenir la muerte, a vivir* (to prevent death, to live). This gesture is a potent example of the diffusion of criminal violence into practices of care. It is not a form of fatalism but a figurative mode in which ideas of care and endurance mix with the tangible criminal violence that pervades the everyday. Let me try to explore this further by recalling an incident that occurred in June 2011.

It was a Tuesday, and I was headed to Serenity. As the taxi slowly moved through the jam-packed streets of Iztapalapa I noticed street vendors and pedestrians wearing thick, heavy-looking chains around their necks. I hadn't noticed this in my own neighborhood, the comparatively rich Colonia Roma, when I set off earlier that morning.

When I arrived at Serenity a counselor named Antonio unlocked the building's imposing metal gate for me. As usual, the interior courtyard was already bustling with activity: women washed clothes on metal washboards, young children played ball, old men read the newspaper and played dominoes. It was a relaxed atmosphere, and the aromas of cooking food clung to the sticky, summer air. I followed Antonio up a flight of stairs to the second story and watched as he unlocked Serenity's iron gate, its main door, and, finally, a heavy aluminum door. It was a cumbersome process that made passage into and out of the anexo a highly anticipated event.

Inside, the anexados were engaged in their morning physical therapy. After chatting casually with a counselor, I took my usual position in a back corner of the room, where I planned to observe the day's activities. For the first hour I viewed anexados running in circles along the perimeter of the room, lifting weights made out of cement-filled cans, and holding their bodies in challenging poses for extended periods of time. These activities continued as Antonio opened the door, permitting the entrance of two men into the anexo. They carried what looked like a rolled carpet over their shoulders. I watched as they laid the object on the floor and slowly unfurled a thin, young woman with flushed skin. Staring at the woman in disbelief, I heard one of the anexados exclaim, "*Órale,* it's Cesi! Cesi's back!" Electrical tape was ripped off her bound wrists, ankles, and lips. Once released, the woman unleashed a flood of obscenities at her abductors and Antonio. When she was finished screaming, she sat against the wall opposite from me, held her head in her hands, and cried.

The scene shocked me, immediately conjuring the image of dead and mutilated bodies, often women's bodies, wrapped in blankets. In the lexicon of the drug war, such figures are called *encobijados* (literally "wrapped in a blanket"). Depictions produced by the media have shown these nameless figures in the trunks of abandoned cars, along desolate rural roads, and in mass graves, culminating in what Adriana Cavavero calls "horrorism," a contemporary regime of violence, degradation, and suffering that is both inexpressible and overrepresented.[29] But the usual storyline of narco-violence didn't seem to apply here. I wasn't sure whether something terrible had just happened or how to respond to the situation at hand.

I walked around the perimeter of the room and sat on the floor beside Cesi. I introduced myself softly; she shrugged me off decisively. I remained seated next to her, both of us with our backs against the wall. I watched the anexados finish their exercises and then scrub clean and dry the cracked tile floor with tattered rags. Such ordinariness made the earlier event even more disturbing. Eventually I mustered the will to visit Padrino Francisco in his makeshift office.

He was organizing stacks of disks of anexados' testimonies, which are copied and sold as a form of treatment literature. The exact details of our conversation are a bit fuzzy, given how upset I was, but I remember asking him why Serenity engaged in such a terrible act of violence. Padrino Francisco responded that kidnapping was just how they did things and that it was effective because the person couldn't escape, which is what addicts do. In a subsequent interview, he described how encobijado forced anexados to experience "las fuerzas de tortura y de tormento" (the forces of torture and torment) that ruled their lives. He suggested that the practice captured not only the individual but these forces as well, crystallizing in a sense the anexado's very precariousness. There is a powerful sensory aesthetics at the core of this practice, one that alerts the anexado to the ruinous forces that destroy life in this particular time and place while also awakening them to the resources for life that endure, including shelter and community. In this context, the realism of encobijado no longer represents a self-evident event but is a difficult and disorienting scene that provides terms of critical thought.

After a few more words with Padrino Francisco, I returned to Serenity's main room. Cesi hadn't moved, and the rest of the anexados were seated in the folding metal chairs assembled in neat, forward-facing rows. Their heads were bowed and eyes closed for the daily religious service. Hector, the oldest anexado at that time, stood before the group and recited a prayer. At first I thought the prayer was for Cesi, as sometimes prayers are offered for new arrivals. But as I followed Hector's words, I recognized that he was reciting the solemnity of Saints Peter and Paul. *Defend, O Lord, thy servants, from all dangers both of body and soul.* I soon realized then that it was Saints Peter and Paul's feast day and that the chains I observed around the necks of pedestrians earlier that morning were a symbol of the saints' suffering for their faith. But given everything else I observed that day, I wondered what else those chains made visible.

The Rainy Season

On 26 June 2012, a shoot-out occurred in Mexico City's Benito Juárez International Airport, resulting in the deaths of three airport police officers who were also rival drug cartel members. The next day I returned to Mexico City for a round of summer fieldwork. Terminal Two was still very much a crime scene, and I tried to steer my young daughters' attention away from the masked federal police and their imposing guns. I was struck by the dissonance between their unsettling presence and the sight of families greeting travelers with bright bouquets of flowers, lovers enjoying long kisses.

Our apartment that summer was on a quiet, tree-lined street with stately houses that had been divided into apartments. A few days after my arrival, I took a metro to Iztapalapa. Vendors navigated their way through the crowded aisles hawking pens, batteries, hand sanitizer, and CDs. Padrino Francisco met me at Constitución de 1917, a metro stop commemorating Mexico's progressive constitution. The battered walls of the station were tagged with slogans that read "The Constitution is dead!"

It was raining that day, as is often the case during Mexico City's summer. In the past I experienced the rain as a source of pleasure. I liked having to take cover with throngs of strangers, all of us huddled closely together under the canopies of buildings or the tarpaulin of market stalls, staring silently at the water spilling over the edge. Although a few people would grow anxious and peel off into the street (their spot immediately filled by someone else), it seemed to me that most people accepted, perhaps even welcomed, the chance to stand so close and still. But that day my experience of rain changed. No longer an onlooker, I was drawn into its vortex.

Mexico City is located in a vast valley at an altitude of over 7,300 feet. Built on lakes and wetlands siphoned by the Spanish, it has suffered from severe water shortages and flooding for centuries. At least 5 percent of the city is not connected to the water supply, and one-third of the city lacks regular access to water. During the rainy season, poor areas with inadequate drainage and sewage systems are transformed into "disaster zones," as if the consequences of the season were unexpected. Low-lying neighborhoods contend with flooding, while informal settlements built on along the slopes of surrounding mountains ranges experience landslides.

In 2012, Serenity moved to an isolated, low-lying neighborhood in an effort to evade the municipal sanitation department, which kept citing it for violating federal standards for operating a rehabilitation center for addiction.[30] Previously, Padrino Francisco paid a modest bribe to avoid an infraction, but the citations become too frequent and the bribes too expensive—he couldn't meet their increasing demands.

Our drive to Serenity's new location was surprisingly long. We passed through parts of Iztapalapa that I had never been to or known about, including its industrial zones. There were food-processing and beer-bottling plants and plastics, textile, cigarette, and chemical factories. Standing passengers crammed into microbuses stared wearily out the window as our taxi passed by them. Eventually, we entered a shabby neighborhood of one-story cement houses and pitted asphalt roads. A few of the houses were painted bright, primary colors, but most were stained from pollution and flooding. The streets were nearly empty of pedestrians and businesses. There were, however, a number of small chapels dedicated to San Judas and Santa Muerte, the saints of lost causes and death, respectively.

Serenity's new neighborhood endured regular cutoffs of water and electricity, a hardship that was rarely imposed in the former location. The building lacked a gate, and its walls were badly cracked. From the outside it looked abandoned, except for the same vinyl banner, now tattered, that read "Rehabilitation Center for Alcoholics and Drug Addicts."

That summer, the number of anexados at Serenity was never less than thirty, many of them teenagers. Several were new to Mexico City, having fled the violence that tormented their rural hometowns in the states of Guerrero, Michoacán, and Tamaulipas. One of the recent arrivals was a fifteen-year-old named Lalo who hailed from a small war-torn town close to the US-Mexico border. He had been in Mexico City for only a few weeks when his mother arranged to have him admitted to Serenity. He recalled, "Everyone said the capital is safer and there are jobs and things. I guess it's true, but I can't tell from here. . . . I'm here [in the anexo] because my mother saw all of the *cholos* in our neighborhood and she was afraid. . . . I don't even do drugs or anything like that. I'm just me and that was enough to land me here." Lalo's story of escaping the troubled countryside for the imagined safety and opportunity in the capital corresponds to the rural-urban tension central to *Post Tenebras Lux*. In both cases, the promise of a better future is denied. What remained, at least for Lalo, was a space for waiting. When I asked him how long he expected to be at Serenity, he responded, "I don't know. Maybe until the war is over. But that will be a long time, no?"

The rainy season took a toll on Serenity. The sandbags stacked around the building's exterior walls didn't stop water and sewage from spreading inside. Anexados used buckets and old cans to collect the fetid water, tossing it right back out into the street. The windows, and even the front door, were sometimes left open to enable this work. No one took the opportunity to escape, suggesting there wasn't a better place to escape to. During the heaviest hour of rain, the usual trickle of water that fell from the cracked ceiling turned into a steady steam. Surrounded by wetness, everything in the anexo was damp: skin, clothes, the heavy wool blankets that were used as beds, bread, and paper. Intestinal sickness was more frequent, and anexados were often weak from dehydration, a cruel irony given all the water. Nevertheless, the usual daily activities continued. One of the counselors had an old guitar and strummed calming melodies in the evening.

Serenity was never visited by the sanitation department or threatened with citations. Nor was it visited by any public or private support services that were supposedly in the area responding to the seasonal "disaster." Families rarely visited, probably because they were contending with the same problems. Padrino Francisco called my cell phone each morning, as if sensing my own reluctance to return. Isolated from markets and vendors, there were things he needed me to bring: cigarettes, cleaning supplies, sweet bread—small signs that life went on.

Contemplating Difficulty

A crucial sequence toward the end of *Post Tenebras Lux* shows Siete in the same field from the opening scene where the young girl wandered during an impending storm. Now, Siete stands motionless, and we see the contour of a surrounding forest from his point of view. The perspective of the camera shifts into the interior of the forest, and the trees are shot from below. The protracted stillness of the shot increases the trees' immensity and singularity, but no clear motivation for the image is offered. Eventually, this image of quiet contemplation is ruptured by the unexpected sound of a falling tree, which begins with the fragile splintering of wood and develops into a thunderous crash. The camera remains firmly in place and records the fall of another tree, and another, the aural and visual image of their collapse amplifying the precariousness that has been slowly building throughout the film.

The camera returns to Siete standing alone in the field, staring blankly at the forest before him. The shot is long and still, and we don't know whether he has witnessed the events or imagined it. The perspective of the camera shifts again, and we observe Siete from behind, at a greater distance than before. He places his hands on the sides of his head, covering his ears, and then moves his hands down to his neck. After several moments of grasping, he decapitates himself. The sequence ends with a lingering long take of Siete's disjointed body inert in the field. Seen at a distance, and in grainy, desaturated colors, the image is one I've always struggled to optically register. Yet it's immediately known to me though the overwhelming feeling of shock it stirs in my body.

Perhaps more than any other, the image of the male decapitated body (*el decapitado*) is the degenerate sign of the drug war. But Reygadas offers a rendering in which predictable causality, meaning, and feeling no longer hold. Siete's death is intercalated with falling trees, a possible reference to indigenous logging communities in rural Mexico, long terrorized and exploited by drug cartels and the Mexican government.[31] *Post Tenebras Lux* does not directly address these themes, but in reworking the drug war's key tropes and fusing them with the forest, the film transforms the terms according to which decapitation can be understood. In this sequence, Siete's self-decapitation joins the symbolic violence of the drug war, and with unexpected potential, for precisely at the moment of his suicide the film becomes productive for contemplating the struggle for survival of Mexico's dispossessed and the limits of endurance.

Walter Benjamin's thoughts on cinematic spectacle and the political significance of shock are pertinent here.[32] Recall that Benjamin considered shock the primary experience of urban life in the modern era, which he related to the numbing of the human senses and susceptibility to political manipulation. Similar ideas about the relentless intensity of narco-violence in Mexico and its desensitizing and normalizing effects on its citizens prevail today. But Benjamin theorizes that, as an aesthetic medium that shatters the habits of human perception, shock can also open a space for critical reflection, enabling transformative political potential and new possibilities of community.

The striking scene recounted above demonstrates this potential by visually and viscerally manifesting Mexico's historically specific sensory environment and making it an essential part of its own critical analysis. In an interview about the film Reygadas says (translated here from the Spanish), "I feel myself tied to a context, and a loyalty to the real. It's a reality that I register with pain."[33] Through the images of a collapsing forest and Siete's self-decapitation, Reygadas makes what is real visibly *felt*. Of course, this alone does not necessarily lead to a progressive politics, but the shock of recognition provoked by the scene provides a critical and embodied perspective on Mexico's present reality, one that includes unforeseen possibilities that lie within it.

The anexo offers another lens from which to contemplate these dynamics. Recall Serenity's physical attrition, its slow temporality and techniques of care. These properties of Serenity disclose a historically situated reality, presented here as a collateral afterworld steeped in the prolonged duration of neoliberal reform and criminal violence. But this presentation does not necessarily anchor the anexo or its inhabitants in familiar and unchanging terms. Indeed, much of the work of the anexo is aimed at registering and disrupting the overextended, repetitive, and fixed dimensions of crisis and endurance in Mexico today. In this way, the anexo is more than a consequence of wider social forces, or a mere illustration of a difficult reality. It is a force and a reality itself, and it makes its audience (in this case, the ethnographer) apprehend its potential through the difficulty of its own sensory compositions.

Notes

I thank Julie Livingson, Zoë Wool, Rubén Martínez, and the anonymous reviewers from the *Social Text* collective for their invaluable feedback on the manuscript.

1. Sobchack, "Stop Making Sense."

2. Brooks, "Cannes 2012."

3. Romney, "*Post Tenebras Lux.*"

4. Young, "*Post Tenebras Lux.*"

5. Sobchack, "Toward a Phenomenology of Non-fictional Film Experience," 244.

6. For Cora Diamond ("Difficulty of Reality"), the *difficulty of reality* refers to those experiences that are within the everyday and that appear to us as having an inexplicable and inexpressive value.

7. See, in addition to *Post Tenebras Lux*, Reygadas's feature-length films *Japón* (2003) and *Batalla en el Cielo* (*Battle in Heaven* [2005]).

8. Guerrero Gutierrez, "Epidemias de violencia." Unless otherwise noted, all translations are my own.

9. I refer here to international guidelines on human rights, ethical and evidence-based medicine, health and safety codes, and liberal approaches to harm, suffering, and recovery that frame these discussions at the level of the individual.

10. Anthropology is increasingly drawing on film as an alternative space to explore social and cultural matters, expand social theory, and develop new modes of ethnographic writing. See, e.g., Fischer, *Emergent Forms of Life*; Ginsburg, Abu-Lughod, and Larkin, *Media Worlds*; Pandian, *Reel World*; and Povinelli, *Economies of Abandonment.*

11. See, e.g., Berlant, *Cruel Optimism*; Herlinghaus, *Violence without Guilt*; and Povinelli, *Economies of Abandonment.*

12. For more on violence in contemporary Mexican film, see Raschotte, *Narco Cinema*; and Tompkins, *Experimental Latin American Cinema.*

13. For more on fabulation in cinema, see Chow, *Sentimental Fabulations*; Deleuze, *Cinema 2*; and Nyong'o, "Little Monsters."

14. Rancière's notion of aesthetics and the indistinction he advances between art and nonart are pertinent here. See esp. Rancière, *Politics of Aesthetics*, 35–37.

15. Voss, "Film Experience," 139. See also Marks, *Skin of the Film.*

16. Rancière, "Aesthetics against Incarnation," 185.

17. Povinelli, *Economies of Abandonment.*

18. Duménil and Lévy, *Crisis y salida de la crisis*; Lapatí and González de la Rocha, "Crisis, Restructuring, and Urban Poverty in Mexico."

19. For a more detailed account of this history, see Garcia, "Serenity."

20. The fee is equivalent of twenty to forty US dollars. It is important to acknowledge the variation in practices in anexos and that not all utilize violence. That said, all of the anexos that I studied employed violence, including involuntary commitment, physical abuse, and confrontational dialogue, as therapeutic techniques.

21. Marks, *Skin of the Film.*

22. Astorga, *El siglo de las drogas*, 2005

23. Heinle, Molzahn, and Shirk, "Drug Violence in Mexico," 37.

24. The precise meaning and usage of *cholo* vary in different times and places. Under the Spanish caste system in colonial Mexico, it referred to a person of mixed Spanish and indigenous ancestry. Today, it has negative connotations associated with ethnic and social class, youth, and criminality.

25. De Luca, "Carnal Spirituality."

26. See Clark et al., "Exporting Obesity."

27. Mateos and Aguilar, "Socioeconomic Segregation in Latin American Cities."

28. Ochoa, "Not Just the Rich."

29. Cavavero, *Horrorism.*

30. These standards include specific facility and procedural requirements, availability of professional medical and psychosocial treatment, and respect for the human rights and dignity of patients.

31. Many of these communities have resorted to *autodefensas* (armed citizen self-defense groups) as a way to endure, leading to charges that they are in collusion with criminal organizations. See Heinle, Molzahn, and Shirk, "Citizen Security in Michoacán."

32. See esp. Benjamin, *Arcades Project*; and Benjamin, "On Some Motifs in Baudelaire."

33. Koza, "Carlos Reygadas."

References

Astorga, Luis. 2005. *El siglo de las drogas.* Mexico City: Plaza y Janes de Mexico.

Benjamin, Walter. 1999. *The Arcades Project.* Translated by Howard Eiland and Kevin McLaughlin. Cambridge, MA: Belknap Press.

Benjamin, Walter. 2006. "On Some Motifs in Baudelaire." In *Walter Benjamin: Selected Writings*, vol. 4, *1938–1940*, translated by Harry Zohn, 313–55. Cambridge, MA: Belknap Press.

Berlant, Lauren. 2011. *Cruel Optimism.* Durham, NC: Duke University Press.

Brooks, Xan. 2012. "Cannes 2012: *Post Tenebras Lux* Review." *Guardian*, 24 May.

Cavavero, Adriana. 2009. *Horrorism: Naming Contemporary Violence.* New York: Columbia University Press.

Chow, Rey. 2007. *Sentimental Fabulations: Contemporary Chinese Films.* New York: Columbia University Press.

Clark, Sarah, Corinna Hawkes, Sophia Murphy, Karen Hansen-Kuhn, and David Wallinga. 2012. "Exporting Obesity: US Farm and Trade Policy and the Transformation of the Mexican Consumer Food Environment." *International Journal or Occupational and Environmental Health* 18, no. 1: 53–65.

Deleuze, Gilles. 1989. *Cinema 2: The Time-Image.* Translated by Hugh Tomlinson and Robert Galeta. Minneapolis: University of Minnesota Press.

De Luca, Tiago. 2010. "Carnal Spirituality: The Films of Carlos Reygadas." *Senses of Cinema*, no. 55. www.sensesofcinema.com/2010/feature-articles/carnal-spirituality-the-films-of-carlos-reygadas-2/.

Diamond, Cora. 2003. "The Difficulty of Reality and the Difficulty of Philosophy." *Partial Answers: Journal of Literature and the History of Ideas* 1, no. 2: 1–16.

Duménil, Gérard, and Dominique Lévy. 2007. *Crisis y salida de la crisis: Orden y desorden neoliberales.* Mexico City: Fondo de Cultura Económica.

Fischer, Michael. 2003. *Emergent Forms of Life and the Anthropological Voice.* Durham, NC: Duke University Press.

Garcia, Angela. 2015. "Serenity: Violence and Inequality on the Edge of Mexico City." *Medical Anthropology Quarterly* 29, no. 4: 455–72.

Ginsburg, Faye, Lila Abu-Lughod, and Brian Larkin. 2002. *Media Worlds: Anthropology on a New Terrain.* Berkeley: University of California Press.

Guerrero Gutierrez, Eduardo. 2012. "Epidemias de violencia." *Nexos*, 1 July. www.nexos.com.mx/?p=14884.

Heinle, Kimberly, Cory Molzahn, and David A. Shirk. 2015. *Citizen Security in Michoacán*. Building Resilient Communities in Mexico: Civic Responses to Crime and Violence, edited by David A. Shirk, Duncan Wood, and Eric L. Olson. Washington, DC: Wilson Institute.

Heinle, Kimberly, Cory Molzahn, and David A. Shirk. 2015. *Drug Violence in Mexico: Data and Analysis through 2014*. Edited by the University of San Diego Department of Political Science and International Relations. San Diego: University of San Diego.

Herlinghaus, Hermann. 2008. *Violence without Guilt: Ethical Narratives from the Global South*. New York: Palgrave Macmillan.

Koza, Roger. 2013. "Carlos Reygadas." *La Voz*. 15 August. www.lavoz.com.ar/ciudad-equis/carlos-reygadas-se-me-acusa-revelar-mi-intimidad-como-si-sabanas-fueran-sagradas.

Lapatí, Agustín Escobar, and Mercedes González de la Rocha. 1995. "Crisis, Restructuring, and Urban Poverty in Mexico." *Environment and Urbanization* 7, no. 57: 57–75.

Marks, Laura. 2000. *The Skin of the Film: Intercultural Cinema, Embodiment, and the Senses*. Durham, NC: Duke University Press.

Mateos, Pablo, and Adrían Guillermo Aguilar. 2013. "Socioeconomic Segregation in Latin American Cities: A Geodemographic Application in Mexico City." *Journal of Settlement and Spatial Planning* 4, no. 1: 11–25.

Nyong'o, Tavia. 2015. "Little Monsters: Race, Sovereignty, and Queer Inhumanism in *Beasts of the Southern Wild*." *GLQ* 21, nos. 2–3: 209–48.

Ochoa, Rolando. 2012. "Not Just the Rich: New Tendencies in Kidnapping in Mexico City." *Global Crime* 13, no. 1: 1–21.

Pandian, Anand. 2015. *Reel World: An Anthropology of Creation*. Durham, NC: Duke University Press.

Povinelli, Elizabeth. 2011. *Economies of Abandonment: Social Belonging and Endurance in Late Liberalism*. Durham, NC: Duke University Press.

Rancière, Jacques. 2004. *The Politics of Aesthetics: The Distribution of the Sensible*. Translated by Gabriel Rockhill. London: Contiuum.

Rancière, Jacques. 2008. "Aesthetics against Incarnation: An Interview with Anne Marie Oliver." *Critical Inquiry* 35, no. 1: 172–90.

Raschotte, Ryan. 2015. *Narco Cinema: Sex, Drugs, and Banda Music in Mexico's B- Filmography*. New York: Palgrave Macmillan.

Reygadas, Carlos. 2012. *Post Tenebras Lux*. Mexico City: Mantarraya.

Romney, Jonathan. 2012. "*Post Tenebras Lux*." *ScreenDaily*, 23 May.

Sobchack, Vivian. 1999. "Toward a Phenomenology of Non-fictional Film Experience." In *Collecting Visible Evidence*, edited by Michael Renov and Jane Gaines, 241–54. Minneapolis: University of Minnesota Press.

Sobchack, Vivian. 2014. "Stop Making Sense: Thoughts on Two Difficult Films from 2013." *Film Comment* 50, no. 1: 51.

Tompkins, Cynthia. 2013. *Experimental Latin American Cinema: History and Aesthetics*. Austin: University of Texas Press.

Voss, Catherine. 2011. "Film Experience and the Formation of Illusion: The Spectator as 'Surrogate Body' for the Cinema." *Cinema Journal* 50, no. 4: 139.

Young, Neil. 2012. "*Post Tenebras Lux*: Cannes Review." *Hollywood Reporter*, 24 May.

Fady Joudah, *Aphrodite's Tunnel*. Courtesy of the artist

Social Text 130 · Vol. 35, No. 1 · March 2017
DOI 10.1215/01642472-3727948 © 2017 Duke University Press

Planetarium

Solmaz Sharif

sign reading CHOOSE LIFE
sign reading SOLVE THE WATER CRISIS
sign reading WARNING UNEXPLODED SHELLS
sign reading DATE SHAKES
which did not mean as we guessed
shaking the palm trees until the dates fell
but what came out of a blender
We are like aliens we say
how best to describe this to the Counselors
and can you believe our luck when out
to watch the stars the dark
interrupted by a boom that is not thunder
a flash that is not lightning from over
the low nearby mountain
but is of course the Air Force Base
running tests or training or regardless
I wanted to write about stars for once and looking
at them thought *My God* thought
This is just like a planetarium
thought of the glow in the dark stars
I stuck all over my bedroom
when between the explosions
it was dark enough

Social Text 130 · Vol. 35, No. 1 · March 2017
DOI 10.1215/01642472-3728044 © 2017 Duke University Press

Footnotes in the Order of Disappearance

Fady Joudah

That syphilis leads to deafness isn't enough
for Beethoven to have died of it. There's Baudelaire
and Nietzsche's tempo, or did Emily Dickinson
suffer from seizures? Did Muhammad? If so

was hers absence and his partial complex? Far less
likely the grand mal type since horror makes itself known.

Dear reader, how might two authors with differing epilepsies write?
Make a documentary on postictal testimony. On bleeding
George Washington to death as part of his treatment plan.

Those who were afflicted with collagen disease
have already been alluded to in a previous book.
Construct an ibid.:

After presiding over mosquitoes Walter Reed pulled a Houdini.
King Louis's anal fistula was heaven-sent
for surgical technique. It was likely during combat
that Sultan Baibers acquired a tear in his pupillary sphincter.

Her eyes were blue her iris orange.
JFK's adrenal disease, that bronze we took for gold, and Lord
Jeffrey, my smallpox Lord.

Social Text 130 · Vol. 35, No. 1 · March 2017
DOI 10.1215/01642472-3728056 © 2017 Duke University Press

As for Familial Mediterranean Fever it belongs to everyone.
Humanitarian medicine is infectious,
its donors stem cell.

Those who received the body were young. Trauma
practice was young, droning about all that talk
of genius and mental illness in 500 words or so.

Name a schizophrenic on the dream list.
Your favorite Lou Gehrig or *The Madness*
of King George, one of my favorite flicks. I saw it
with a lover I lost, her eyes were hazel, their waters green.

Now repeat after me
the three objects I asked you to hold.

For I never had a cat I called my own.
For he ravaged the neighbor's chickens for monk brains.
For they kidnapped him and he never returned.

Thank You

Fady Joudah

professor who ran the anatomy department and was a preacher's son. You were an ex-preacher yourself, abandoned the cloth after you divorced your wife and married your lover. Thank you for your hands that a surgeon would kill for, your mouth for transfiguration, enunciation, you were kind to me.

At the end of each year you held a memorial service for the cadavers. Afterlife believers or not, they would all be cremated. The fuss about the body interred is not the same as about the body discovered. I threw my name in the hat. I'd recite verses from the Quran in Arabic and then you would follow in English. I proposed and you accepted. I had my own bilingual copy. I forget which verses I chose but they were generous to the faithful. And when my turn came I put on my best Barry White and went into a trance.

"You didn't notice it," my friend later asked me, "the discomfort in the room when you read?" I didn't, I said. All I heard was how the professor read. He was so good. He nailed every syllable, word.

Social Text 130 · Vol. 35, No. 1 · March 2017
DOI 10.1215/01642472-3728068 © 2017 Duke University Press

Bleak House

An Afterword

Elizabeth A. Povinelli

This tightly conceived collection provides us with a luminous set of ethnographic encounters with exhausted social worlds and the effort that people within them exert to create embankments against partial or utter dissolution. Its focus is directed at the concept of *the social*, a term whose dismantling was certainly well under way by the time Hannah Arendt in *The Human Condition* (1958) famously took umbrage at its rise and the subsequent transformation of politics. As Arendt railed against a concept and form of governance organized primarily to enhance the health of a new people—a people which, Michel Foucault argued, were better understood as a population—many indigenous, anticolonial, feminist, queer, black, and brown social movements were denouncing "the Social" for very different reasons. There was no *the Social*, definite article, capital S, although not for the reasons Margaret Thatcher would claim. No singular social existed; rather, there were extractions and distributions that created and then crossed the unequal terrains of various human spaces. True, many still called for a new form of society that would truly enhance the lifeworlds of all.

As neoliberal economics displaced Keynesian imperialism, a new geography of precarity and vulnerability greeted even those who previously benefited. By 2012, the year the authors in this volume first brought their work together in another forum, the forms of abandonments seen during the high-water mark of neoliberalism had given way to the stagnation of the Great Recession. The Bush wars were not won, nor did they end, although the damaged and maimed bodies kept piling up everywhere. And by 2012, the ethnographic magic of conjuring social or cultural reason where others saw none had long given way to the practice of

Social Text 130 · Vol. 35, No. 1 · March 2017
DOI 10.1215/01642472-3728201 © 2017 Duke University Press

conjuring hope where none should be expected—to find poetry where others might read psychosis; decampments in the midst of the most draconian detention centers. The village had long given way to the bleak house as the privileged site for ethnographic reflection.

These essays would certainly seem to be solidly situated within this Dickensian turn. Suicide is a central thematic, as is radical aloneness. And when human bodies are not in the existential grip of social isolation, it is because they are being forcibly socialized in drug detention centers and postwar rehabilitation hospitals. And if we are not contemplating suicide, we are heading straight into the grave or up the maggot-ridden butts of street dogs.

Of course, the residents of the bleak house have long been of interest to social theory; thus, it is no surprise to find the name of Émile Durkheim invoked in the collection's framing. Modern sociology defined itself by claiming it could tell us something more, something truer, about collapsed physiological and psychic states than could the sciences of psychiatry, psychoanalysis, and medicine. Erving Goffman's writing on stigma and the total social institution and Foucault's writings on madness and the clinic are critical moments in this unfolding conversation, as are Catherine Malabou's recent reflections in *Les nouveaux blessés* (2007). There, Malabou explores a double foreclosure that emerges across psychoanalysis and neuroscience when they face certain forms of human injury such as brain trauma and Alzheimer's. Whereas psychoanalysis is silent about these conditions because they are considered physiological rather than psychic states, neuroscience is silent about the psychic conditions and experiences of those experiencing these conditions because they are not considered pertinent to the physical trauma. What sort of theory and rhetoric are needed for an ethical encounter with these forms of existence?

Although none of the essays in this volume explicitly says so, the collection as a whole opens the question of how and what the discipline of anthropology and the practice of ethnography have to say to and about these spaces that seem on the surface so desolate. What role do they have to think with or through these spaces, and what right? What is the purpose of entering and dwelling within them? Something like a set of answers seems to emerge across these essays, or perhaps less a set of answers than a set of problems. The first answer, or problem, is deceptively simple. The reason to dwell critically in these spaces is simply to insist that their existence have a public. And this insistence that these spaces be able to claim space within the public of critical thought is indeed increasingly necessary given the forms of institutional erasure arising from the intersection of legal preemption and liberal "protection." We can think here of the rise of the human subjects institutional review boards, whose purpose and function are stretched across the cynical reason of the university's desire to preempt lawsuits and the liberal goodwill to protect human and non-human animals from the excessive intrusions of the will to know. At this intersection a barricade is raised against knowledge of, with, and within the late liberal distribution of precarity and vulnerability.

Second, the reason to dwell within and with these social worlds is to show that the condition of life within these spaces provides a critical perspective on the formation of late liberal power. If we believe that the governance in, through, and of life defines the form of contemporary power, something we have now long called biopolitics, then the condition of late liberal life (slow death, shattered life, depressed existence) is no longer inside or outside this politics. The vulnerable, the precarious, the depressed, the shattered: what is biopower when these conditions are not the tail ends of the statistical curve of normative life but the peak center? Third, all of these essays remind us that dwelling demands, or is at its heart, a political purpose, and this purpose is to interrupt a given formation of power rather than either report and adjudicate that formation or report and extract an affective charge of hope from it. The rhetorical force is aimed not at feeling for but at affecting with—of staying with the errant rather than trying to quickly press it into a form of resistance, of hope, of an alternative social world.

But what these essays also do—and I think the courage of this needs to be acknowledged—is register the strain, anxiety, and discomfort of trying to treat these social conditions as something other than spaces for adjudication, affective extraction, or liberal intervention even as they show, with rich exacting descriptions, that they exist at the intersection of exhaustion, endurance, and death. Thus, as certainly as the argument of each essay bears careful attention, so does the rhetoric, which is often weirdly factual and decidedly (at least attempting to be) inert to liberal affect.

Anne Allison takes readers into the affective force of a social fact, namely, that many contemporary Japanese men and women are dying alone. The essay rhetorically vibrates with an analytic ambivalence that mirrors, in order to intensify, the social condition of relationality's increasing absence. Note that Allison is not encountering a condition, or a politics, of antirelationality, antinormativity, or counteraction. She is encountering a radical irruption of asociality at the heart of neoliberal sociality and encountering the social practices emerging around and through this hole in sociality. She focuses on the rise of suicide and the emergence of new ways of caretaking the dead. But as Allison braids the fact of high suicide and the increasingly abandoned shrine, her prose strains to follow the optimism of the new mortuary movements that argue that the solitary death can give rise to new forms of collective feminist memorializations and lineal homage. What to do with the facts that these new mortuary movements have an economic logic and interest (how to keep the temple financially viable) and that feminist understandings of the new roles that women play are animated by political concerns? Is it because of these economic and political interests that her essay gives way to the draining existential despair of those youth for whom the question of what to do has given way to the question not merely of why do anything at all but also why exist at all.

This turn on existence versus social form is also found among the men and women in the US military hospitals in which Zoë H. Wool writes an ethnography of trauma. She also finds a form of solitude. And the fragmented conditions of this solitude are also the social alienations of a post-Keynesian world. But here we are shown the materially shattered bodies of an ongoing war and a landscape of defunded care. As with Allison, we find Wool struggling to wrench positivity out of decidedly errant socialities. Much rests on what she describes as the in-during bonds of interned soldiers who evidence intense attachments with one another while within the hospital but do not seem to see a need to extend these intensities outside the hospital grounds or into the future. No matter how it might sound, the phrase "here today, gone tomorrow" is affect neither of the devil-take-care nor of a Broadway show. It is not nihilism or vitalism. What it *is* is what Wool, like Allison, struggles to convey. Note "struggles to convey" as opposed to understand—this form of in-during exists. But that's where Wool thinks we should leave it. Leaving it there allows her to draw a distinction between the consequential and the transformative, allows her to say that in-during bonds are consequential socialities without being transformative socialities, allows her to open a spacing for something that is inside and outside the affective script of an ever optimistic liberalism. In-during bonds do not sink into asociality, but neither do they quite take us forward into a new way of being together.

Lisa Stevenson sketches a deathscape outside of late liberal (biopolitical) ways of recognizing harm and taking care and inside of ongoing settler disruption. Three topological layers are explored. Stevenson begins with the living ghosts produced when, in the 1950s, the settler state removed Inuit children and adults with tuberculosis to southern hospitals. When the children returned they were sometimes greeted as ghosts, parents and relatives not recognizing their children as living, and the children unable to relate to their living relatives. Stevenson knows, of course, how this history of settler care maps onto others, most notoriously the removal of children during the boarding school tragedies. But Stevenson layers into this ghostly landscape another mapping of death, as the Inuit use death to mark place, so that place is narrated through stories of where so-and-so fell and died. And these layers are stitched together through an existential stance toward time and endurance summarized by the phrase "everyone dies" as a bracing counterpoint to liberal hysteria over, supposedly, the preciousness of life when in practice it is often merely the preciousness of certain lives—certainly not Inuit lives. Rather than life and death as ultimate values, Stevenson thinks with the Inuit about the form of living and the where and with whom of dying. I was reminded reading this essay of Rolf de Heer and David Gulplili's 2013 film *Charlie's Country*. In this film, the evacuation of the sick from what is called remote Australia to Darwin Hospital is figured not as a way station to death as an existential abstraction but as a demand to die in a specific way, as if settler colonialism hadn't attempted to impose enough forms of life.

Angela Garcia begins her essay with an explicit film reference, Carlos Reygadas's luminous film *Post Tenebras Lux* (2012), an analytic and aesthetic exploration of the tense relation between contemporary elite and rural Mexicans, and, from within a scene central to the movie, curls into contemporary drug treatment centers (*anexos*) in Mexico City. At the heart of the essay is an attempt to read a movie as something other than an apologia for the contemporary Mexican elite and to encounter contemporary drug treatment centers as something other than vicious manifestations of neoliberal abandonment. They are both also these things, as, Garcia notes, anexos provide a space in which to endure, and possibly subvert, the consequences of marginality and violence typical of contemporary Mexico, but without transcending them. The essay is remarkable in its ability to face the violent practices of some of the anexos without turning this violence into the secret truth of their rotten or redemptive core, their true corruption or poetry. One engages (in) violence not to seek hope and certainty but precisely to disrupt the controlling nature of these affective thoughts.

The experimental space between scholarly and poetic analytics is exemplified in the poetry of Fady Joudah and Solmaz Sharif, brilliant poets whose precise prosody lays bare the signs that cross glow-in-the-dark stars with surgical tables, dog-eared texts, and monk brains. What world is this where date shakes and syphilis, seizures and anal fistulas write a new alien geography? What language will we create and find to light the way?

In the intensity of these essays, maggots are a welcome reprieve. But Naisargi N. Dave's essay is also exemplary of the entire collection's attempt to pay careful attention to the texture of these worlds while remaining inert to liberal affect. Dave takes the reader on a journey around the cycle of life and death as human, cow, dog, and maggot define the topography of existence. There is no purity here, no space where good affect can relax. A man who draws no distinction between forms of life nevertheless barks orders to another man who labors for him. And another man who carefully ministers to a dog's maggot-ridden ass does not express great concern when the now-dewormed canine is nearly hit by a car. Having done what he could do, he does not seem to obsess over what lies beyond his doing—if the dog dies by car accident, so be it. Perhaps another man will take it upon himself to tend to roads as carefully as he tends to intestines. What Dave opens is a space beyond a liberal schoolboy logic in which care is either made a universal ruler or denied altogether. If you cannot do everything—solve the problem across a homogenized space—then why act at all? Dave seems to counter: in overwhelmed worlds one does something or doesn't, and these are consequential but not universal actions.

References

Arendt, Hannah. (1958) 1998. *The Human Condition*. Chicago: University of Chicago Press.

Malabou, Catherine. 2007. *Les nouveaux blessés: De Freud à la neurologie, penser les traumatismes contemporains*. Paris: Bayard.

Printed and bound by CPI Group (UK) Ltd, Croydon, CR0 4YY

13/04/2025

14656479-0002